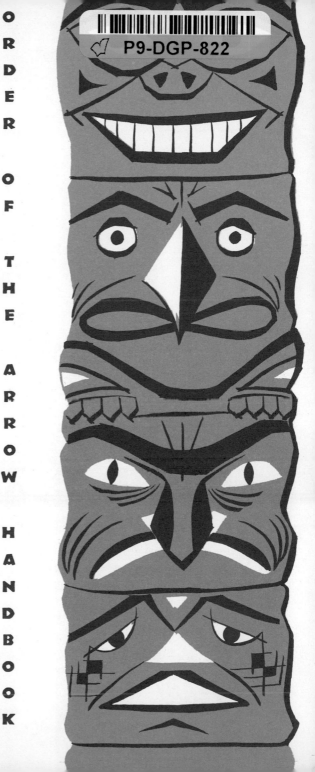

ORDER OF THE ARROW HANDBOOK

P9-DGP-822

ORDER OF

THE ARROW

Copyright 1965
BOY SCOUTS OF AMERICA
North Brunswick, New Jersey
No. 5000   Printed in U.S.A.   110M870

CONTENTS

MY ORDER OF THE ARROW MEMBERSHIP RECORD

My name _____

Address _____

I became an Ordeal member on _____

date

In the _____ Lodge

name and number

    at _____

place

I became a Brotherhood member on _____

date

    at _____

place

I became a Vigil Honor member on _____

date

    at _____

place

My Indian name is _____

which means _____

I have held these offices in my lodge _____

_____

_____

_____

_____

I have attended these area and national conferences _____

_____

_____

_____

_____

FOREWORD

We proudly present this edition of our *Order of the Arrow Handbook*. What a satisfaction it has been to see the little acorn, planted in 1915, grow to be the stalwart oak in the forest of Scouting, thriving in every State of our Nation.

That this growth has occurred is the result of no one man's work. Over the years, there have been thousands of men, young and old, who with great devotion have given themselves to the development of the Order of the Arrow. Members of our national committee, present and past – two of whom have risen to the office of Chief Scout Executive; an illustrious band of national and area conference chiefs; and above all that earnest group of local lodge advisers and chiefs–all of these and countless others, whose names are unknown, have played a part in the nourishment and growth of our stalwart oak.

From the beginning it has been our hope that the Order would serve a useful purpose in causing the Scout Promise and Law to spring into action, especially in the Scout camps in all parts of our Nation. We are still dedicated to that high purpose.

Beyond that, as we have pointed out in previous editions of this handbook, there are certain arrow points to the successful operation of the Order which should be recognized. Here they are.

The Order of the Arrow is a *thing of the individual* rather than of the mass. In our scheme, each individual is important. This has always been stressed in our Order. Indeed, certain of our ceremonies were developed with particular boys in mind. The very ideals of brotherhood, cheerfulness, and service spring to life in the flesh-and-blood appearance of real individuals. Yes, in the Order each member is important, for what each one does counts in establishing the Order's success.

Such an idea is basic to our democracy, just as it is offensive to totalitarians.

The Order of the Arrow is a *thing of the out-of-doors* rather than the indoors. It was born on an island wilderness. It needs the sun and the rain, the woods and the plains, the waters and the starlit sky.

We pick up the lore and tradition of the American Indians and glorify them today. The Indian was a lover of the open air and his culture is ours to preserve.

It is to be hoped that one of our greatest achievements will be the strengthening of the Scout movement as an out-of-door experience. In this respect we have a double task:

We have a quantity job to do, for still too large a percent of our troops and posts are not camping.

We have a quality job to do to secure genuine camping that produces self-reliance in the individual camper.

For out of life in the open comes a precious ingredient which our country and any country needs if it is to survive–self-reliance that makes men strong in any time of stress.

The Order of the Arrow is a *thing of the spirit* rather than of mechanics. Organization, operational procedure, and paraphernalia are necessary in any large and growing movement, but they are not what count in the end. The things of the spirit count–

Brotherhood–in a day when there is too much hatred at home and abroad.

Cheerfulness–in a day when the pessimists have the floor.

Service–in a day when millions are interested only in getting or grasping rather than giving.

These are of the spirit, blessed of God, the great divine spirit.

It is to these ideals that this handbook is dedicated. May its pages serve you well as you go forward in brotherhood and cheerful service to God and your country.

E. Urner Goodman

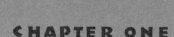

CHAPTER ONE

HISTORY, PURPOSE, AND PRINCIPLES

The Order of the Arrow was founded during the summer of 1915 at Treasure Island, the Philadelphia Council Scout camp. Dr. E. Urner Goodman was camp director and Carroll A. Edson his assistant. These two men, working with their staff at Treasure Island, originated the ideas that became the basis for this nationwide campers honor society of the Boy Scouts of America. Goodman later had a distinguished career in the professional service of Scouting, serving as Scout executive in Philadelphia, then Chicago, and later as national director of the Program Division. Edson served in Scouting for a number of years then entered public service work in New York State.

The directors of the Philadelphia camp found that it was desirable to have some definite form of recognition for those Scouts who best exemplified the spirit of the Scout Oath and Law in their daily lives. Since the valley of the Delaware was rich in Indian tradition and the site of the Scout camp was an island used in bygone days as a camping ground of the Lenni Lenape or Delaware tribes, it seemed only natural to base this campers honor society on the legend and traditions of these Indians.

In the beginning, the organization was known as the Wimachtendienk W.W., but later as the Order of the Arrow. The first meetings and ceremonies were held in a wooded part of the island not generally used for the camp activities. In this secluded spot, the founders built a council ring where all honors, including promotions in Scout rank, were awarded. As the highest camp honor, Scouts previously chosen by the members of each of the troops at the end of their stay in camp were called out before all the campers as candidates for the Order. After the public ceremonial, those candidates who had previously undergone an ordeal of hard work, silence, and scant food for one day were then admitted into the Order of the Arrow.

Friday, July 16, 1915, dawned bright and clear on Treasure Island. In addition to the heavy heat which often hangs over the valley of the Delaware, there was something else in the air. It was an almost indescribable feeling of expectancy and mystery.

While only a few of those on the island had been taken into the confidence of the leaders, everyone in the camp was aware that this was the big night, although very few had any idea what was to take place. Everyone waited with

2

an interest and an enthusiasm that were difficult to control. The day wore on slowly.

By sundown the air was charged with a tense excitement that cannot be described. But those who were present will remember it as an experience never to be forgotten. Something that was to be a vital factor in the lives of uncounted boys and men was about to be started. The importance of this undertaking was unconsciously exerting a strange influence on all of those present.

As darkness fell the campers were lined up in a single file by Harry Yoder, who acted as guide and guardian of the trail. In dead silence the campers followed the guide by a circuitous route through the woods to the site of the council fire. The path led under a great fallen tree, and the council ring was so located that as the boys approached the fire they were unaware of its existence until they had passed down a small ravine across which an old fallen tree lay.

Suddenly the council fire was revealed, built in a triangular shape, behind which stood the co-founders of the Order of the Arrow—E. Urner Goodman, Chief of the Fire, and Carroll A. Edson, Vice-Chief of the Fire. Both were wearing long black robes, the chief with a turtle superimposed upon a triangle, which denoted leadership, and the Vice-Chief of the Fire, then called Sachem, wore on his robe a turtle without the triangle. (The turtle is the totem of the Unami Lodge.)

The original ceremony was quite different from that which developed later. There were three lessons taught that night:

1. The candidate attempted to encircle a very large tree, individually, with outstretched arms. Having failed, he then was joined by several of the brothers who together had no difficulty encircling the large tree, thus teaching lesson No. 1, BROTHERHOOD.

2. The candidate was directed to endeavor to scale a steep bank at the edge of the council ring. Failing, he was again assisted by the brothers with whose help he was able to climb the elevation, thus teaching SERVICE.

3. The candidate was then given a bundle of twigs and told to place some on the council fire, where the twigs caught fire and blazed brightly, thus showing CHEERFULNESS.

From the day of its founding in 1915, the Order of the Arrow has been an influence for good in the camping program of Scouting. It has always recognized those Scout campers who best exemplified the Scout Promise and Law in their daily lives. It has developed and maintained camping traditions and spirit, and at all times promoted Scout camping.

But perhaps of greater importance than the above is the fact that the Order of the Arrow has had an enormous influence for good on the lives of thousands of boys and young men by helping to crystallize the constant habit of helpfulness into a life purpose of leadership in cheerfulness to others.

From that time forward the Order of the Arrow has been centered in the camping program not only in its original setting at Treasure Island but in hundreds of councils of the Boy Scouts of America. Now there are over five hundred lodges, and the Order of the Arrow is accepted as an important segment of the camping program.

From 1915 until 1921 the Order grew slowly. World War I kept Scouts and leaders busy with many other problems and projects. In 1921 steps were taken to establish the Order on a national basis. The early years had produced sufficient experience to form a foundation on sound basic policies.

The first national convention was held on October 7, 1921, in Philadelphia, at which a national lodge composed of four delegates from each of the local lodges was formed. This group adopted a constitution and a statement of policies. Committees were appointed to develop plans for making the Order effective as a national campers honor society.

Following the convention there was a steady growth in lodges and membership. At the suggestion of the national lodge, meeting in Reading, Pa., the Order of the Arrow became an official program experiment of the Boy Scouts of America in 1922.

For several years conventions of the national lodge were held each year. After 1927, they were held at 2-year intervals. During the Philadelphia convention of 1929, it was suggested that the Order become an official part of the Boy Scouts of America and a component part of its program. At the session of the national lodge in 1933, held at the Owasippe camps of the Chicago Council, this proposal was made and ratified by the delegates.

On June 2, 1934, at the National Council Meeting of the Boy Scouts of America, in Buffalo, the Order of the Arrow program was

4

approved by the National Council.

In May 1948, the National Executive Board of the Boy Scouts of America, upon recommendation of its Committee on Camping, completely integrated the Order of the Arrow as a part of the program of the movement. The national lodge of the Order was dissolved. The Order's national supervision came within the regular administrative channels of the Boy Scouts of America.

Thus, the executive committee of the national lodge became the national Committee on Order of the Arrow, a subcommittee of the national Committee on Camping and Conservation. A staff member was employed as national secretary in the Camping and Conservation Service of the Program Division at the home office to handle administrative duties under the direction of the national director of the Camping and Conservation Service.

A number of great Scouters were prominent in the evolution of the Order of the Arrow. Former Chief Scout Executive Arthur A. Schuck served as national treasurer in 1921 and became national chief in 1922. Joseph A. Brunton, Jr., past Chief Scout Executive, served as national chief from 1938 to 1939. Special mention is made of H.

PURPOSE OF THE ORDER

To recognize those campers—Scouts, Explorers, and Scouters—who best exemplify the Scout Oath and Law in their daily lives and by such recognition cause other campers to conduct themselves in such manner as to warrant recognition

To develop and maintain camping traditions and spirit

To promote Scout camping, which reaches its greatest effectiveness as a part of the unit's camping program, and to help strengthen the district and council camping program both year around and in the summer camp, as directed by the camping and activities committee of the council

To crystallize the Scout habit of helpfulness into a life purpose of leadership in cheerful service to others

Lloyd Nelson, secretary for 9 years, chief for 4 years, and national chairman for 6 years. His service to the Order of the Arrow was second to none.

The Order of the Arrow emphasizes that a good Scout camper is not only proficient in the skills of Scoutcraft but also practices the principles of Scouting expressed in the Scout Oath and Law and in the tradition of the Good Turn. Particular attention is paid to cheerful service as an essential to a happy camping experience. True brotherhood exists among those who exhibit these traits in their daily lives.

The Order as you can see from the statement of purpose is not a program or a thing apart from Scouting.

It is a device used in the camping program of the Boy Scouts of America.

It has its roots in the troop and post that goes camping.

It gathers those designated by troops or posts as members of the Order into a local council group known as a lodge.

It is natural that the program and setting of Scout camping should lead to the formation of campers honor societies. In the early years of Scouting in America many such organizations were formed. The success of the Order of the Arrow in its early expansion years was due in large measure to the democratic basis for the selection of candidates; the recognition of the Scout unit; the camping requirement; a practical plan for service to Scouting in which the promotion and improvement of camping, beginning in a boy's own unit, were the central idea; colorful ceremonies; a well-defined plan of organization; literature—covering ceremonies and administration—that could be easily adapted to local councils; the practical and colorful interpretation of the Scout Oath and Law; the Good Turn and the spiritual qualities of Scouting.

The growth of the Order of the Arrow through the years has never been based on an aggressive promotional plan. It came because councils believed in the ideals expressed by the Order and voluntarily requested that lodges be formed. The soundness of providing a single workable campers honor society, rather than many, is evident. Over 700,000 Boy Scouts, Explorers, and Scouters have been inducted into the Order during the past 50 years. There are now over 250,000 active members in 508 local lodges. This coverage of the Nation makes possible a unified approach. It provides for transfer of membership, standard books and supplies, national training plans, and a coordinated scheme for building strength in local units through regional and national service. All of these add color, enthusiasm, and quality to the camping program of Scouting.

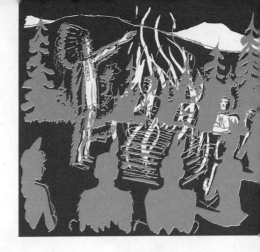

Principles of the Order

The Order exists primarily as a service organization and especially emphasizes cheerful service in the camping part of the program. It is democratic in character. Boys are elected to membership by the members of their own Scout troop or Explorer post. They elect their own officers, plan their own program, and carry out service projects under their own leadership. Adults act as advisers and counselors but do not run the affairs of the local lodges. Membership is granted to boys and adults on the basis of "not so much for what they have done but for what they are expected to do" in service to their fellowmen.

Membership in the Order stems from the home unit and serves to strengthen a member's responsibility to his own unit rather than to draw him away in another program of activities and service projects.

The Order of the Arrow is not a secret society. An air of mystery does surround its ceremonies and meetings, but this is done because of its appeal to boys. Boys who are nonmembers should not be permitted to attend Ordeal, Brotherhood, or Vigil ceremonies. Scout leaders, clergymen, educators, parents, and others who wish to know the full story of the Order may easily find the answers to their questions by inquiring through their council office.

Spiritual values in the Order of the Arrow seek to glorify the principles of a Scout's duty to his God, country, and fellowman.

Membership in the Order is contingent upon membership in the Boy Scouts of America. Members wishing to be active in the Order must maintain their registrations.

7

CHAPTER TWO

RELATIONSHIP TO SCOUTING

The Order becomes most effective when Scouts or Explorers are chosen by members in their own unit. They are well known to each other as a result of their camping experiences and other unit activities. Since the Order is closely related to camping, its members must remember that the ideal method of Scout camping is their chartered unit camping under its own leadership either on or off the council site.

The Order and the unit

This statement, written by E. Urner Goodman, the founder of the Order, makes it clear that its purpose has always been to strengthen the Scout or Explorer in his relations to his own unit:

"Let it be remembered that the Order of the Arrow was created to help the unit—to help it set before its membership a better idea of the inner qualities of the good Scout camper.

"Thus it is that each unit is asked to select one or more of its members who have set such an example and to designate them as its representatives in a brotherhood of cheerful service. The happiness and welfare of the unit camp depend upon these quali-

ties fully as much as upon such skills as camp cookery and camp sanitation. There is often a relationship between a clean latrine and cheerful service!

"And mark you this: qualities of character, like cheerfulness and service are hard for à boy, or a man, to understand in the abstract. They come easier when seen in human life.

"So the Order was started to help glorify these qualities of the good Scout camper in the unit, so that they might be appreciated there, not only during the all too short term in camp, but through all of the days and the weeks of the year.

"Now the older the Order becomes, the larger we grow, the more we need to remember the significance of the Order in the individual unit. It seems logical and proper that lodges should arrange their procedure so that units camping 'on their own' might designate their representatives to the Order just as readily as units camping at the council camp.

"By all means then, let us realize the significance of the Order in the unit—for the unit is still our one best hope in Scouting, even as the family is still humanity's chief hope."

The Order and the local council

An Order of the Arrow lodge is an integral part of the camping and activities program of the local council. The council camping and activities committee has a direct relationship to the operation of the lodge. The lodge adviser, who is appointed by the Scout executive, serves as a member of the camping and activities committee to coordinate the program of the lodge with the objectives of his committee. The camping and activities committee chairman may also appoint one of his men to serve with the executive committee of the Order. In this way, the lodge, helping to improve and promote camping, becomes a strong right arm to the committee.

The Order and the district

A number of lodges have been organized on a chapter basis covering one or more districts in the local council. In this situation an adult adviser may become a member of the district camping and activities committee and works closely with the district organization to ensure the effectiveness of the chapter.

The Order and the service area

An Order of the Arrow service area consists of from six to eight local councils and is served by a deputy regional Scout executive, a member of the national staff of the Boy Scouts of America, who serves as regional adviser to the area. Another deputy regional Scout executive on each regional staff serves as coordinator of Order of the Arrow affairs within the entire Scouting region.

Once a year, or at least every 2 years, representatives of the lodges in this service area come together for an area fellowship training conference that presents a splendid opportunity for learning more about the Order. The only function of this area organization is to plan and conduct successful fellowship training conferences.

The area adviser is a professional Scouter, usually the Scout executive of one of the councils in the area. He is appointed by the regional office to act as a kind of Order of the Arrow commissioner for the several lodges in the area. He works closely with the area conference chief and the area leader to make sure that the area training conference is a success. He may be called upon as an expert consultant on Arrow affairs within the area, to help reorganize dropped lodges, and to interpret all national Order of the Arrow policy.

11

THE ORDER OF THE ARROW
AND ITS PLACE IN SCOUTING

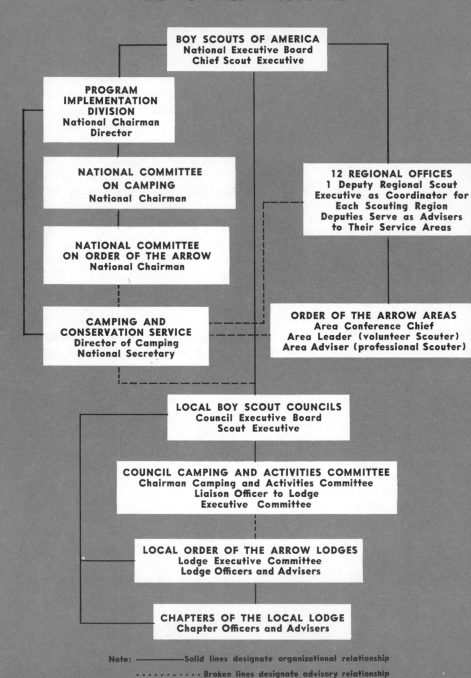

BOY SCOUTS OF AMERICA
National Executive Board
Chief Scout Executive

PROGRAM IMPLEMENTATION DIVISION
National Chairman
Director

NATIONAL COMMITTEE ON CAMPING
National Chairman

NATIONAL COMMITTEE ON ORDER OF THE ARROW
National Chairman

CAMPING AND CONSERVATION SERVICE
Director of Camping
National Secretary

12 REGIONAL OFFICES
1 Deputy Regional Scout Executive as Coordinator for Each Scouting Region
Deputies Serve as Advisers to Their Service Areas

ORDER OF THE ARROW AREAS
Area Conference Chief
Area Leader (volunteer Scouter)
Area Adviser (professional Scouter)

LOCAL BOY SCOUT COUNCILS
Council Executive Board
Scout Executive

COUNCIL CAMPING AND ACTIVITIES COMMITTEE
Chairman Camping and Activities Committee
Liaison Officer to Lodge
Executive Committee

LOCAL ORDER OF THE ARROW LODGES
Lodge Executive Committee
Lodge Officers and Advisers

CHAPTERS OF THE LOCAL LODGE
Chapter Officers and Advisers

Note: —————Solid lines designate organizational relationship
· · · · · · · · · ·Broken lines designate advisory relationship

The area leader, a volunteer Scouter who is appointed by the regional office, is responsible for the area conference, at which a local lodge acts as host. The area conference chief, a member under 21 years of age for his entire term of office, is elected by the lodges in his area. He works with the volunteer area leader in directing the planning for the meeting. (Pages 67-73 of chapter 6 give details for planning and conducting the area fellowship training conference.)

Our national committee

The National Order of the Arrow Committee is a subcommittee of the Committee on Camping and Conservation. Committee members are appointed by the President of the Boy Scouts of America and the Chief Scout Executive. Each of our 12 Scout regions is represented on the committee that meets from time to time to coordinate the program of the Order throughout the country. The national secretary is an assistant director of the Camping and Conservation Service. He works directly under the national director of the Camping and Conservation Service in the Program Implementation Division of the Boy Scouts of America at New Brunswick, N. J.

The Order of the Arrow is fully integrated into the camping program of Scouting across the Nation as the official campers honor society of the Boy Scouts of America.

International use of the Order

In keeping with the principle that the Order is a program device in Scouting and not an organization in itself, the policy is that other Scout associations are free to use the plan on their own. It is further understood that no organizational responsibility exists between the Order of the Arrow as it functions in the Boy Scouts of America and the Order's program as it may be used abroad. International responsibility rests with The Boy Scouts World Bureau as do all international relationships in Scouting.

CHAPTER THREE
MEMBERSHIP

To become a member of the Order of the Arrow a Scout or Explorer is chosen by vote of the boys in his unit. This is a unique feature of the Order since the majority of those who select their candidates for this honor are not members of the lodge. However, lodge members in the unit have a vote just as do nonmembers. In this way membership is controlled by boys in their own units and not by those who are already Arrow members.

It is important that the members of the unit have the requirements to become a candidate properly explained. Elections should never become a popularity contest. Candidates should be chosen on the basis of being a true Scout or Explorer and a qualified camper.

Boy membership requirements

These are the qualifications for a boy to become a member of the Order of the Arrow:

1. UNIT LEADER APPROVAL. To become eligible for election a Scout or Explorer must have the approval of his unit leader. The leader must certify as to his Scouting spirit, his adherence to the Scout Oath and Law, and participation of each nominee. He must also certify that the nominee meets all specified requirements.

*2. CAMPING REQUIREMENT. A Boy Scout or Explorer must have 15 days and nights of camping under the auspices and standards of the Boy Scouts of America. The 15 days and nights must include one long-term camp (6 consecutive days and nights for Boy Scouts or 5 consecutive days and nights for Explorers) within the 2-year period prior to election. The balance of the 15 days and nights must be made up of short-term (overnight, 2-, 3-, or 4-day) camps.

*3. UNIT QUOTA. Election to the Order is by the home unit. Each unit may hold only one election per year within a period officially designated by the lodge. The number of candidates a unit may elect shall be based on the total registered active membership of the unit at the time of the election. If a troop or post has any Eagle Scouts who are not members of the Order of the Arrow, these Eagles may be elected in addition to the quota. Eagle Scouts do not become candidates for Order of the Arrow membership automat-

*Asterisk indicates a revision of requirements that become effective January 1, 1969. The revisions are optional until then.

ically; they must still have their unit leader's approval and must meet all the specified requirements. In the event that the Eagles do not receive enough votes to appear within the unit's quota, they are not elected. Scouts of lesser rank may not be substituted for the Eagle Scouts in case the Eagles are not elected.

4. WHO MAY VOTE. Every registered active member of the unit under age 21 at the time of the election is eligible to vote. Fifty percent or more of the unit membership must be present to hold an election. In voting for candidates for the Order of the Arrow, unit members should make their choices in terms of fellow members who have demonstrated in camp and elsewhere a spirit of cheerful service for the common good.

*5. FIRST CLASS REQUIREMENT. A Scout has 6 months to attain First Class rank from the date of election. He must be First Class at the time of induction into the Order. There is no rank requirement for Explorers, but they must have been registered active members

*ORDEAL NOMINATIONS

Total active unit membership at date of election	Number of candidates that may be elected
- 5	1
6 - 14	2
15 - 24	3
25 - 34	4
35 - 44	5
45 - 54	7
55 - 64	8
65 - 74	9
75 - 84	10

of an Explorer post or Scout troop for at least 6 months prior to election.

If a Scout does not meet the First Class requirement within 6 months of his election, the election is void. He may, however, be reelected by his troop at the next election. A troop may hold an Order of the Arrow election without having any First Class Scouts within its ranks. Normally, a candidate will be inducted no more than 6 months after his election.

Exception to the 6-month requirement can be made by action of the lodge executive committee in case of illness or other suitable reason.

*6. METHOD OF ELECTION. The election shall be held in the following manner: The name of all unit members eligible for the election shall be posted in alphabetical order on a blackboard or large sheet of paper; each member of the unit will then list the names of the candidates he believes to be best qualified in the order of his preference (first choice, first; second choice, second; etc.), as shown in the following example. The Scoutmaster or Explorer Advisor and at least one Order of the Arrow member tally the ballots. Candidates with the highest scores are those elected for membership in

the Order of the Arrow. Example: There are 27 troop members, 23 are present for the election. Seven boys are qualified campers, are approved by their Scoutmaster, and are eligible for election. The troop is entitled to elect four candidates. The names are posted alphabetically:

Bill	Harry
Charles	John
Dick	Tom
George	

Each troop member is given a ballot; he writes down the numbers 1 to 4 and then writes the names of four boys in the order of his personal preference.

Example: 1. John 3. George
2. Dick 4. Bill

Since the troop may elect four candidates, those listed first are given 4 points; those second, 3 points; third, 2 points; and fourth, 1 point. Those with the four highest scores are elected for membership in the Order. In case of a tie for last place, a runoff election is held in the same manner, listing only those who are tied and permitting troop members to make the final choice between the two members who are tied. In case of a tie for first, second, or third, those who are tied will be elected. There will be no fourth place. In other words, the four boys with the four highest scores are elected. In the event that there are Eagle Scouts who are running for election, the Eagles' names must appear within the troop quota. This situation will entitle the troop to have one additional candidate for each Eagle Scout who is elected within the quota. For example: A troop has 10 members eligible for election and is entitled to elect 4 of them to Order of the Arrow membership. There are two Eagle Scouts in the troop who are not now members of the Order. The qualified members are listed in alphabetical order:

Albert	John
Bill	Kenneth
*Charles	Lawrence
George	*Marvin
Harry	Walter

*Charles and Marvin are Eagle Scouts. When the preferential balloting is completed, the boys are listed in this order:

Unit Quota
1. Walter	6. Bill
*2. Charles	7. George
3. John	*8. Marvin
4. Albert	9. Harry
5. Lawrence	10. Kenneth

Number 5, Lawrence, is elected as Eagle Scout Charles' election does not count against the quota. Number 8, Marvin, is an Eagle Scout but he is not elected. In the event that Marvin had placed fifth, then the troop would be permitted to have the top six boys as candidates for Order of the Arrow membership.

*7. ANNOUNCEMENT OF RESULTS. As soon as the election is completed, the Scoutmaster must announce the names of members who have been elected to the entire troop. Names and addresses of the newly elected candidates must be forwarded to the lodge membership committee immediately. Candidates will be called out or tapped out at the earliest possible time, either at a camporee or a special ceremony or at summer camp. Lodges can arrange to conduct a tap out ceremony at the troop or post meeting immediately after the election.

8. INDUCTION. To be inducted into the Order the candidates must participate in the Ordeal and the Ordeal ceremony.

9. NO VOTE FOR SCOUTERS. Adult Scouters (over 21 years of age) may not vote in boy elections. These requirements may not be changed in any way by the local lodge.

Scouter elections

Since the Order of the Arrow is principally a boys' organization, Scouters are not elected to membership as an award or recognition.

Election to the Order should take place when the Scouters' job in Scouting will make Order of the Arrow membership more meaningful in the lives of boy members.

Scouters' qualifications are the same as those of boy members; however, the camping requirement may be waived at the discretion of the lodge executive committee.

Scouters of a unit holding an election for boy members may select one of their adult members, provided he meets the camping requirement (15 days and nights of Scout or Explorer camping including one long-term camp).

Unit, district, and council Scouters may (with the approval of the lodge and staff advisers) be invited by the lodge executive committee to be candidates for induction to membership.

Members of the local council professional staff are members ex officio of the local lodge. If they haven't been previously inducted into the Order, they should be given an early opportunity to take the Ordeal and Ordeal ceremony.

Informing units of elections

At a time of year determined by the lodge policy, the troop and post leaders are mailed a letter announcing elections.

Holding the election

At a time and place determined after reading the letter, the Scouts or Explorers of the unit assemble with their unit leader to elect candidates.

When a unit leader is a member of the Order, he will explain to the group the "Purpose of the Order of the Arrow," outline the basis on which candidates should be selected for this highest camping honor, and describe the method of election on page 18 of this manual. If the unit leader is not a member of the Order, a member of the Order should be delegated by the lodge chief, with the leader's consent, to make this presentation and assist the unit leader with the election.

After the purpose of the Order is read and explained to the group preparing for the election of the candidates, they can be trusted as Scouts or Explorers who best know their fellow campers in their unit to make the right selections.

Executive membership

The Scout executive, camp director, assistant camp director, and such other professional staff members designated by the Scout executive are members ex officiis of the local lodge, and when newly

Sample Letter Announcing Elections

TO: UNIT LEADERS
FROM: ORDER OF THE ARROW, W.W.W. LODGE NO.___
SUBJECT: UNIT SELECTION OF CANDIDATES

The Order of the Arrow is a campers honor society chartered by the Boy Scouts of America. Its purpose is to recognize those campers who best exemplify the Scout Oath and Law in their daily lives and, by such recognition, cause other campers to conduct themselves in such a manner as to warrant similar recognition; to promote Scout camping and develop and maintain its traditions and spirit; and, finally, to crystallize the Scout habit of helpfulness into a life purpose of leadership in cheerful service to others.

Each Scout troop or Explorer post with qualified Scouts, Explorers, and Scouters is urged to hold an election not later than _____ to select candidates for an Ordeal to be held at _____ on _____. The date of the election is selected by you as unit leader. A member of the Order of the Arrow will be on hand to help with the election. Units with 5 registered active members may elect 1 candidate; 6 to 14, 2 candidates; 15 to 24, 3 candidates; 25 to 34, 4; 35 to 44, 5; etc. If there are any Eagle Scouts in the unit who are not members of the Order, their election within the above quota will give the unit one additional candidate for each Eagle Scout elected.

SCOUT OR EXPLORER QUALIFICATIONS

1. Any Scout or Explorer registered as an active member of his unit may, with the approval of his unit leader, be nominated for election.

2. A SCOUT CAMPER is defined as a Scout or Explorer who has completed at least 15 days and nights of

21

camping under the auspices of the Boy Scouts of America during the 2-year period prior to the election. The 15 days and nights must include one long-term camp (6 consecutive days and nights for Boy Scouts, 5 consecutive days and nights for Explorers). The balance of the camping must be overnight, weekend, or other short-term camps.

3. There is no rank requirement for a Scout or Explorer to be elected. For induction a Scout must be First Class rank. He has 6 months to complete his First Class requirements from the date of the election. An Explorer of any rank may be inducted.

SCOUTER QUALIFICATIONS

1. Any Scouter camper registered actively in a chartered unit of the council is eligible.

2. A Scouter must meet the same camping requirement as Scouts and Explorers. One Scouter may be elected by the other Scouters registered with his unit. In order to hold an adult election the unit must have conducted an election for boys.
   Voting for candidates will be based on their spirit of brotherhood, cheerfulness no matter how tiresome their duties, and a willingness to give unselfish and wholehearted service to others at all times.
   A return postcard is enclosed for you to use in notifying the Scout office of the date set aside for the election of candidates. It should be held at a regularly scheduled Scout meeting. Every effort should be made to have 100 percent attendance of both Scouts and Scouters. A member of the Order will help your leaders with the election.

Scoutingly yours,
Lodge Chief

appointed, if they have not previously been inducted into some lodge of the Order, should be given an early opportunity to take the Ordeal and the Ordeal ceremony. Camp staff members are to be elected by members of their own unit or, if they are council or district Scouters, they should be elected by the lodge executive committee.

The Scout executive is the Supreme Chief of the Fire of the local lodge and, with the council camping and activities committee, has full responsibility for the entire program of the lodge.

Candidate status

After election, a Scout, Explorer, or Scouter remains a candidate until he takes the Ordeal of the Order. If this period of candidacy exceeds 6 months, his name is dropped and he is no longer a candidate. To become a candidate again, he must be re-elected. The executive committee of the lodge may extend the 6-month period between election and induction if a candidate is ill or there are other unusual circumstances.

Ordeal membership

The steps in working toward Ordeal membership are clearly defined. After a person has been *elected* to the Order by his unit members he is formally recognized as a candidate at a calling

out ceremony conducted by a team of Arrowmen. If he is qualified for induction, he takes part in a brief pre-Ordeal ceremony, then an actual Ordeal or series of tests of his sincere dedication to the principles of the Order, and is finally accepted in a colorful Ordeal ceremony.

This sequence is explained in detail in this chapter which also covers the later requirements for Brotherhood and Vigil Honor membership that come as a result of personal growth over a period of years in the Order.

Calling out ceremony

Many lodges have developed a type of calling out ceremony for camp use and vary it, accord-ing to their own wishes. It is sometimes done at the evening parade in the camp; at a special gathering of all the Scouts, Explorers, and Scouters in the camp; in the dining hall at dinner; or on some other suitable occasion. Kichkinet, a member of the ceremonial team, often appears in costume before the assembled camp, bearing to the successful candidates written messages or some symbolic emblem indicating their election. This recognition can be used to impress the other Scouts and Explorers in camp with the solemnity and purpose of the Order.

Calling out ceremonies have also been developed for other than summer camp use at camporees and district and council events, and for individual units at one of their hiking or camping sites.

If the pre-Ordeal and Ordeal ceremonies are to be held during the night and day following the "calling out," the candidates are instructed by an Ordeal master about how to prepare for them. If some time is to elapse before these ceremonies, the following information should be sent to the candidate by mail:

Official notice that the candidate has been selected by his fellow campers to membership in the Order of the Arrow.

Specific date, place in camp, and time at which he should report for the Ordeal. (When it is possible, a full year's program of lodge activities, including all scheduled Ordeals, should be enclosed with the letter.)

Instructions that the candidate come fully prepared with blankets or sleeping bag and a ground cloth for an overnight camp-out alone in the open. (When the Ordeal is held during the summer camp season, food may be supplied from the camp commissary. Otherwise, advise the candidate about the cost of food and the name and address of the Ordeal master whom he must notify that he is coming so that food may be furnished by the lodge. Another method is to provide the candidate with a list of items he must bring himself.)

Ordeal master's job

The Ordeal master is appointed by the lodge chief with the advice and consent of the Scout executive, camp director, and lodge adviser to have charge of the candidates during the pre-Ordeal and the Ordeal. He must be a member with mature judgment, and have full authority to make substitutions in the normal Ordeal procedure to cope with varying circumstances—severe weather conditions, a candidate's illness, or some physical infirmity. No candidate's health should ever be endangered by undermining his bodily resistance or by exposing him to any hazardous situation.

The Ordeal master is responsible for seeing to it that the Ordeal is conducted on a high standard with no hazing. He must be extremely careful that each candidate fully understands the symbolism of the pre-Ordeal ceremony and the reasons for all of the Ordeal tests to which he is subjected—spending the night alone in the open to prove his courage and ability; maintaining silence to better study his inner thoughts and resolve upon a life of richer service in the future; spending some time at hard work to prove his willingness to serve; eating but little to prove he can subordinate the appetites of the body to the high purpose of the spirit.

The entire pre-Ordeal and Ordeal should, if possible, be conducted in some place not usually visited by Scouts or Explorers and the candidates kept reasonably separated from other campers. No effort should be made deliberately to tempt a candidate to break his pledge of silence or to eat more food than officially authorized by the Ordeal master. The Scout executive, camp director, and the Ordeal master and his assistants who help conduct the Ordeal have authority to suspend the requirement of silence when urgent needs arise or discussion periods are scheduled and will notify the candidates when the silence is to be resumed.

Approved ceremonies

Pre-Ordeal and the Ordeal ceremonies are printed in full in the *Ordeal Ceremony* pamphlet, No. 5005. All ceremonies of the Order are prescribed nationally. They have been printed after close check and approval by the Institutional Relationships Division and with the various religious groups. No change of any kind is, therefore, permitted to be made in the set ceremonies by any local lodge of the Order. Hazing and blindfolds are forbidden in all Order of the Arrow ceremonies.

The ceremonial team

The ceremonial team consists of four members to take the speaking parts for the pre-Ordeal and Ordeal ceremonies. Additional members as desired by the local lodge may serve as caretakers of the council fire, assistant guides, and the like.

All who take part in the ceremony should be dressed in appropriate Indian costume. Other members attending join in the circle of membership, in Scout or Explorer uniform, and wear the Arrow sash. All help preserve the solemnity of the occasion.

It is of the utmost importance that the members of the ceremonial team have their speaking parts thoroughly memorized and their movements carefully rehearsed. Since the pre-Ordeal and Ordeal ceremonies are the new member's first real knowledge of the meaning of the Arrow, he should receive an impression that will be a constant inspiration to him to participate actively and grow in the service of the Order.

CEREMONIAL TEAM

Mighty Chief	Allowat Sakima
Medicine Man	Meteu
Guard	Nutiket
Guide	Kichkinet

Pre-Ordeal ceremony site

If possible, a secluded place to the north of the camp, used for no other purpose, should be chosen for the short pre-Ordeal ceremony. It should be given after dark but not so late that it encroaches upon the proper time for sleep. The candidates should then, as part of their Ordeal, be assigned alone to separated safe places to camp in silence for the night.

The Ordeal

The purpose of this Ordeal is to have the candidate meet the four tests expressed in the pre-Ordeal ceremony—sleeping apart, silence, work, and scarcity of food.

This is the Ordeal plan:

The candidate sleeps alone in a selected spot for one night.

AT 6:30 a.m. the candidate is awakened and given the chance to bathe and pack his belongings.

AT 7:30 a.m. he is given a breakfast of one egg sandwich and one cup of cocoa or, as a test of his camping ability, he may be required to prepare this meal himself. If he has an allergy to eggs, he may be allowed to substitute some other item of food. It is the Ordeal master's responsibility to see that each candidate has sufficient food at breakfast and lunch to carry him through the work of the morning and afternoon but not so much as to prevent his meeting the test of eating but little. Allow time after breakfast for cleaning up and taking a short rest period.

AT 9:30 a.m. there is work of service to others. The candidate undertakes carefully selected but not too laborious camp projects such as improvements of camp, building or repairs to ceremonial grounds, care of other property assigned to the lodge, and such. The work may be carried out by all the candidates working together on one project or the group may be split among several projects, depending upon how many candidates there are and the type of projects selected. The projects must be worthwhile so that the candidates will have a feeling of accomplishment. Such work should not be a part of the ordinary camp chores—nor distasteful work. Neither should it be work ordinarily undertaken by your camp custodians. All such work is done—according to Ordeal custom—in silence.

At 11:30 a.m. is the cleanup, followed as soon as possible by the first discussion period on the significance of the Ordeal. Candidates are permitted to ask questions of the Ordeal master and to speak sufficiently to learn each other's names. Then there is a return to silence, and each candidate has the opportunity to carve some symbolic emblem—such as the totem of the lodge or an Arrow —to exchange with his fellow candidates as a memento of their common experience.

AT 1 p.m. is lunch, consisting of one sandwich and one large cup of milk. This is followed by a brief rest period.

AT 2 p.m. the service work for others, started in the morning, is continued.

AT 4:30 p.m. there is a second discussion period. Candidates may again break the silence to take part in the discussion. This is one of the most valuable aspects of the Ordeal and should be conducted by the Scout executive, camp director, or their selected deputy. It offers a splendid opportunity for character-development guidance.

This discussion may cover the pre-Ordeal ceremony and the Ordeal up to this time. The candidates should be asked to give their interpretations of why the various elements have been included in the ceremony and the Ordeal and should understand the symbolism of the ceremony.

The discussion is concluded by the Ordeal master who again imposes silence and announces that the candidates will be permitted to have a full evening meal and will be dismissed until the time of the Ordeal ceremony when they will complete their induction. They are reminded that what has occurred to them is of no concern to anyone else. Candidates then rest in preparation for the ceremony.

Compliance with the Ordeal

When the election of candidates, the pre-Ordeal ceremony, and the Ordeal up to this time have been conducted on a Scout-like basis, there is no reason why all candidates should not have met all the test of the Ordeal.

One time in a thousand there may be such a flagrant violation of the spirit of the Ordeal as to suggest that a candidate is unworthy. In this instance the candidate usually withdraws without being prompted, because he realizes his own shortcomings.

However, the Ordeal master should report any such violations to the Scout executive or camp director who may discuss the matter privately with the candidate involved. The members of the lodge, it must be remembered, have no vote as to the acceptance of a candidate properly elected by his fellow campers.

The Ordeal ceremony

The Ordeal ceremony should be given sufficiently early at night to permit the candidates who have been through an arduous mental and physical test to get sufficient sleep. It is held on the ceremonial grounds prepared as shown in the illustration on page 6 of the *Ordeal Ceremony* pamphlet. Preferably it is a separate setting reserved for the purpose, and may be the same area used for the pre-Ordeal ceremony or a different one.

Local lodges have made their ceremonial grounds places of beauty; not only through the work of the Ordeal candidates but by long and continuous volunteer service by the members.

After the ceremony

Many lodges have all of their members—old and new—assemble in another place immediately after the Ordeal ceremony to have a short social meeting with light refreshments so that they may all become better acquainted. This planned period of comparatively quiet fellowship serves to avoid a letdown after the beauty and impressiveness of the Ordeal ceremony.

Either at this fellowship meeting or the next morning, the officers of the lodge or their deputies should get the correct names, addresses, etc., from the new members for the lodge records; collect their dues; and present them with their Ordeal insignia, neckerchief, membership card, and a copy of the *Order of the Arrow Handbook* and the Brotherhood questionnaire. Requirements for Brotherhood should then be explained to all new Ordeal members so that they can properly prepare themselves to seal their membership in the Order after 10 months or more service as Ordeal members.

Brotherhood membership

After a period of about 10 months to 1 year, during which the new Ordeal member has shown a continued interest in Scouting and the camping program and has served others cheerfully, he may seal his membership in the Order of the Arrow by participating in the Brotherhood ceremony.

"Not so much for what you have done as for what you are expected to do"—this we learned in the Ordeal ceremony. Recognition comes for our first efforts, but we are expected to continue to serve.

The Ordeal and Ordeal ceremony brought to the new member many ideas and ideals that were new and difficult to comprehend. During the year that follows, he is able to think about his induction into the Order and how he has tried his best to live according to the principles that were taught him.

The Brotherhood affords him an opportunity to continue with a life of cheerful service to others and to strengthen those things that were taught in the Ordeal. These two elements make up the complete induction into membership and, after the Brotherhood ceremony, the member becomes a "brother" in the lodge. The Order is trying, thereby, to impress upon the new member the value of a life of cheerful service to others and the knowledge that all others are his brothers.

The Ordeal consists primarily of physical impressions, new associations, and additional preparation. The Brotherhood ceremony is one of deeper and quieter mental impressions for the member.

Brotherhood eligibility

Every Ordeal member who meets the following qualifications is given the opportunity for induction as a Brotherhood member:

- Ten months service as an Ordeal member.
- Registered active membership in Scouting.
- Registered active membership in the lodge.
*• The candidate for Brotherhood must know the Order of the Arrow Obligation and the "Order of the Arrow Official Song." He must be able to answer all the questions in the Brotherhood questionnaire in a satisfactory manner.
*• Before taking the Brotherhood ceremony he must submit a written statement regarding his rededication to the principle of cheerful service to his fellowmen. This statement of 100 to 200 words is submitted to the Brotherhood ceremony committee before the Brotherhood ceremony.

When an Ordeal member meets these standards he may seal his membership in the Order. It is up to the Ordeal member to decide

Sample Letter Announcing Brotherhood Eligibility

Dear Ordeal Member:

It has been at least 10 months since your induction into Ordeal membership in our lodge of the Order of the Arrow.

If you have continued faithfully to serve your fellowmen and have completed the stipulated requirements, you may now seal your membership in the Order through the Brotherhood ceremony.

- Ten months service as an Ordeal member.

- Registered active membership in Scouting.

- Registered active membership in the Order of the Arrow.

- Know the answers to the questions in the Brotherhood questionnaire including memorization of the Obligation and the "Order of the Arrow Official Song."

Before going through the ceremony you must submit a written statement of 100 to 200 words expressing your rededication to the principle of cheerful service to your fellowmen. "He alone is worthy to wear the Arrow who will continue faithfully to serve his fellowmen."

Your first opportunity will be at the Brotherhood ceremony to be held at (specify place, date, and time). If you are prepared now to make this important decision for yourself, we will welcome you at the ceremony. Please let us know of your intention so preparations can be made for all those who will attend.

_____, Secretary

_____ Lodge

31

whether or not he wishes to participate in the Brotherhood ceremony. A letter similar to the one on page 31 should be sent to all Ordeal members when they have completed 10 months or more of service as an Ordeal member.

Conducting the Brotherhood ceremony

The ceremony for Brotherhood membership is printed in full in the *Brotherhood Ceremony* pamphlet, No. 5006.

Each candidate for Brotherhood should have been given the Brotherhood questionnaire upon the completion of his Ordeal ceremony. Just before the cermony a committee of Brotherhood members will satisfy itself that all the members to be inducted are familiar with the aims and purposes of the Order of the Arrow and the Ordeal as outlined on the question sheet.

If he does not have an acceptable knowledge of the answers to the questions, he should be allowed more time for study. It is not necessary for him to learn the answers word for word as long as he can correctly interpret them in his own words. If the candidate is unable or unwilling to answer, his induction should be deferred until he is prepared.

The "Order of the Arrow Official Song" and the Obligation must, however, be memorized.

At a time and place determined by those responsible, the Brotherhood ceremony may be held, as outlined in the *Brotherhood Ceremony* pamphlet. It is desirable to conduct the ceremony in camp. Only candidates and Brotherhood members should attend.

Purpose of Brotherhood membership

From the inception of the Order in 1915, it was intended that all its members should be of the same rank or standing. Brotherhood membership does not carry with it any degree of rank, status, or special privilege within the lodge. It is not to be thought of as a separate honor in the same sense as the Vigil Honor. Except for making the necessary arrangements for Brotherhood ceremonies, it is not necessary for Brotherhood members to meet as a separate group. Social and service activities are not held for Brotherhood members apart from other members of the lodge.

The Brotherhood is an opportunity for members to evaluate their past contributions to Scouting and the lodge and to reaffirm their belief in the high purposes of the Order. The ceremony is intended as a source of inspiration, motivating its members to render even greater service to Scouting.

The Vigil Honor

The Vigil Honor is the highest honor that the Order of the Arrow can bestow upon its members. It dates back to the year 1915, when its founder, E. Urner Goodman, became the first Vigil Honor member. Since then, thousands of members have been accorded this honor.

It is a high mark of distinction and recognition reserved for those Scout, Explorer, and Scouter members of the Order who, by reason of exceptional service, personal effort, and unselfish interest, have made distinguished contributions beyond the immediate responsibilities of their position or office to one or more of the following: their lodge, the Order of the Arrow, Scouting, or the Scout camp. Under no circumstances should tenure in Scouting or the Order be considered as ample reason for Vigil Honor recommendation.

Vigil Honor members have an honorable tradition to uphold. They must at all times conduct themselves in accordance with the ideals of Scouting, the Order of the Arrow, and the Vigil Honor.

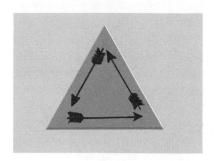

Membership cannot be won by a person's conscious endeavor. It comes as a recognition of his altruistic leadership in service. This fact should be given careful consideration in the selection of candidates for membership. The Vigil Honor has successfully fulfilled a very definite and satisfactory service to the Order of the Arrow, to Scouting, and to the individual members. Its continued success depends on the care with which future members are selected and on the maintenance by its members of the high ideals of service to others for which the Vigil Honor has always been known.

Any member of the Arrow registered in Scouting and in good standing in a regularly chartered lodge is eligible for recommendation to the national committee for elevation to the Vigil Honor, provided that at the time of his recommendation he has been a Brotherhood member for a minimum of 2 years. Since the Order of the Arrow is primarily a boys' organization, it is suggested, in recommending candidates for the Vigil Honor, that preference be given to those who have become members of the Order as Scouts, rather than those who have been taken into the Order as adult volunteer or professional Scouters.

Members of the Order can be inducted into the Vigil Honor only with the written approval of the National Order of the Arrow Committee.

Choosing Vigil Honor candidates

Local lodges should use the following procedure in recommending candidates for the Vigil Honor and in carrying out the Vigil Honor induction. The lodge chief appoints a Vigil Honor nominating committee of three or more members who are approved by the lodge adviser and the Scout executive. The committee members should be Vigil members; however, any member of the lodge may serve on the committee. The local lodge Vigil Honor nominat-

ing committee then uses the following step-by-step procedure in determining their Vigil Honor nominations to be submitted to the national committee for approval.

1. Secures from the lodge secretary a complete list of Brotherhood members who are actively registered with the lodge and the Boy Scouts of America and who have been Brotherhood members for at least 2 years.

2. Determines the number of Vigil Honor candidates that the lodge is eligible to nominate to the national committee by finding how many members were reported on the latest charter renewal application of the lodge.

Since Vigil Honor candidates are nominated only once a year, there can be no possibility of duplicating the count of members.

This procedure was set by the National Order of the Arrow Committee in order to maintain the Vigil Honor standards.

Nominations of professional Scouters, presidents of councils, and council chairmen of camping and activities committees will not count against the lodge quota. Men in this group will, of course, have to meet the requirement of at least 2 years' service as Brotherhood members.

34

3. In selecting candidates to be nominated for the Vigil Honor, keep these qualifications in mind:

a. Candidates must have been Brotherhood members for at least 2 years.

b. When weighing "distinguished service" in nominating candidates, remember to measure it on a boy standard for boys and on an adult standard for adults.

c. To maintain a proper ratio of boys to men in awarding the Vigil Honor, the national committee will not approve petitions for more than 50 percent of adults during any given year. All candidates may be boys, but not more than 50 percent may be adults. (Adult is interpreted as a person 21 years of age or over.)

4. Select the Indian name and English equivalent for the candi-

*VIGIL HONOR NOMINATIONS

Total lodge membership reported on latest charter renewal application January 31 of current year.	Maximum number of Vigil Honor nominations
0 - 49	1
50 - 99	2
100 - 149	3
150 - 199	4
200 - 249	5
250 - 299	6
300 - 349	7
350 - 399	8
400 - 449	9
450 - 499	10
Ratio of 1 to 50	

date. Pages 116-21 provide some Indian-English translations from the Lenni Lenape language.

5. Prepare the Vigil Honor Petition—National Record Cards. These cards can be secured through your council office from the national secretary.

The petition must be filled out completely before it can be approved. Particular care should be used in furnishing membership figures requested on the back of the card and in giving the month, day, and year that the Brotherhood was conferred. Specific reasons for nominating the candidate for the Vigil Honor should be concisely but completely listed.

6. Secure approval of the petition from the local lodge executive committee and the Scout executive. The lodge chief and the Scout executive or assistant must personally sign the back of the card before approval can be given.

7. Forward the Vigil Honor Petition—National Record Card with the Vigil Honor fee of $1 for each candidate to the national secretary. Make the check payable to the Boy Scouts of America. If the petition is not approved, the fee will be returned.

Thirty days must be allowed for the national committee to consider the petition and advise the lodge of its acceptance or rejection.

8. Upon receipt in the national office, the petitions will be reviewed for approval. If approved, the certificates will be sent to the council Scout executive. If petitions are not approved, the council Scout executive will be notified with an explanation for the disapproval or a request for further information if it is needed by the national committee.

9. When approval of the candidate is received, arrange and conduct the calling out ceremony for the Vigil Honor candidate. There is no standard form for this and local lodges are encouraged to work up their own.

10. Order Vigil Honor sashes from the Supply Division of the Boy Scouts of America through your local council office.

11. Arrange and conduct the Vigil Honor induction. If there are no Vigil Honor members in the lodge, arrange to have candidates inducted by a nearby lodge or bring in Vigil Honor members from another lodge to conduct the induction.

12. Arrange and conduct a public presentation of the Vigil Honor sashes and certificates to the new Vigil Honor members at some major function of the council or the lodge. Because the Vigil Honor is a recognition for exceptional leadership in service, it is important that an appropriate presentation be made.

13. If approved candidates are not inducted, it is very important to notify the national secretary of the Order immediately. Otherwise, they will be considered inducted members of the Vigil Honor, and their cards will be kept on permanent national file.

Distinguished Service Award

The National Order of the Arrow Committee presents the Distinguished Service Award to those who have rendered outstanding service to the Order on an area, regional, or national basis. It is given primarily for service to the Order and Scouting over a long period of time.

The committee seeks to maintain an equal balance between young men and adults over 21. Recommendations for this award are made through the 12 regional offices. Awards are presented at national conferences of the Order of the Arrow held every 2 years.

Red Arrow Award

Individuals who are not members of the Order of the Arrow may be recognized by the national committee for outstanding service to the Order. In 1967 the committee established the Red Arrow Award for this purpose. This award in the form of an engraved plaque with a red arrow superimposed is only presented through action by the national committee. Recommendations in writing should be presented to the committee for consideration through the national secretary. The awards are presented in connection with the national conferences of the Order of the Arrow.

CHAPTER FOUR

ORGANIZATION

Since the Order of the Arrow is an official part of the Scouting program it is essential that the Scout executive recognize it as one of the program features within the council. It is his responsibility to see that it functions in a satisfactory manner.

The Scout executive is the Supreme Chief of the Fire in the Order of the Arrow. He appoints a volunteer Scouter as lodge adviser or Deputy Supreme Chief of the Fire. This appointment is made in consultation with the chairman of the council camping and activities committee. This lodge adviser assists the Scout executive in supervising the operation of the lodge program and serves as a member of the council camping and activities committee.

In some councils the Scout executive acts as staff adviser but in most he appoints a member of his staff, usually his camp director or assistant Scout executive as staff adviser, Chief of the Fire, to act for him in giving guidance to the lodge.

The title of Camp Chief of the Fire is used to designate the camp director.

Adult role in the Order

The local lodge is the important unit within the Order. It is here that the program operates. The Order of the Arrow is a camping program device with its

LODGE ADULT ADVISERS

Supreme Chief of the Fire	Natami Gegeyjumhet	Scout executive
Deputy Supreme Chief of the Fire	Witawematpanni Gegeyjumhet	Lodge adviser
Chief of the Fire	Nischeneyit Gegeyjumhet	Director of camping or assistant Scout executive—staff adviser
Camp Chief of the Fire	Nacheneyit Gegeyjumhet	Camp director

LODGE ADVISER'S ROLE IN THE ORDER

- Acts as a keyman in bringing about a successful administration of an Order of the Arrow lodge.
- Is coach and counselor to the elected officers of the lodge.
- Is a member of the council camping and activities committee and acts as official representative of the local council in coordinating its affairs.
- Works closely with the staff adviser and the lodge chief.
- Attends all lodge meetings, ceremonies, and activities.
- Is a member of the executive committee and gives direct guidance to the lodge chief and officers.
- Consults with the officers on plans for lodge projects and activities.
- Provides for the training of new officers and a smooth transition from one administration to the next.
- Keeps lodge affairs on a high plane and in harmony with the principles of Scouting and national policies of the Order of the Arrow.
- Promotes participation of his lodge in area fellowship conferences, national training courses, and national conferences.

activities in the field of camping. It fulfills this purpose only when it is properly administered. Several adults imbued with the purpose of the Order should give leadership to it; not directly as officers but by guidance and coaching, leaving the direct leadership to the elected officers of the lodge.

In most of the outstanding and successful lodges we find the lodge and staff advisers acting as coaches. They are like the football coach. They know the rules of the game, how to pass, run, kick, and tackle.

The coach knows some good plays and knows how to run inter-ference. He knows how to block a punt and how to weld his players into an effective team.

Once in a while the coach has to make a substitution. He sometimes calls in the captain or the quarterback and talks turkey to him and sometimes he has to tell a fellow to go take a shower.

The good coach schedules skull sessions with his team and gets their opinions and suggestions on how to get the ball across the goal line.

The coach is a vital necessity in the game of football just as are the advisers in an Order of the Arrow lodge.

In the game of football and in

STAFF ADVISER'S ROLE IN THE ORDER

- Works closely with the lodge adviser and the lodge chief. These three are responsible for the successful operation of the lodge.

- Assumes the responsibility for maintaining the Order of the Arrow in its proper relationship with all other segments of the council program.

- Keeps the members of the local council staff informed and advised on activities of the lodge and seeks their understanding and support.

- Encourages cordial relations between all Scouters of the council and the Order of the Arrow lodge, especially the members of the camping and activities committee.

- Advises the lodge officers on national procedures and policies of the Order and, thereby, helps maintain harmony within the lodge.

- Helps to pave the way for unit membership elections through training courses, roundtables, and other meetings of Scouters.

- Coordinates the Order of the Arrow program in summer camps and works with the camp director and camp staff in stressing the need for cooperation between Arrowmen and camp staff in planning the camp program.

- Makes arrangements with the council office for the clerical services needed by the Order—setting up a proper bookkeeping and accounting system, arranging for the use of office equipment, typewriters, mimeograph machines, and files.

- Brings to the attention of the executive committee of the lodge the names of nonunit Scouters who should be considered for election to membership in the Order.

the game of the Order of the Arrow the boys carry the ball and play the game. The coaches or the advisers are not on the field, but the quality of the teamwork and the skill of the players are a direct reflection of the ability of the coaches or the advisers.

The success of Scouting over the years can be credited to the wonderful volunteer Scouters who continue to give leadership, companionship, and guidance to over 3½ million American boys.

Sure the Order of the Arrow is a boy operated outfit, but remember it's the coaching that makes the difference.

In maintaining the leadership of the lodge in the hands of boys, the importance of the role of the adult advisers cannot be over-emphasized. Adults are in a key position to bring about and maintain an able lodge administration and ensure the successful operation of the lodge. They should look upon their membership in the Order as another opportunity to give guidance to boys and to help them to develop their leadership abilities.

Baden-Powell said in his *Aids to Scoutmastership,* "Scouting is a game for boys, under the leadership of boys, in which elder brothers can give their younger brothers healthy environment and encourage them to healthy activities such as will help them to develop citizenship."

Scouter candidates must always remember that the Order is a boys' organization, and that a Scouter's election to membership should not be used as a recognition or an award. A Scouter should be elected only when his job in Scouting will enable him to make the Order of the Arrow more meaningful in the lives of boys.

Local lodge boy officers

The elected officers of the lodge are the lodge chief or Netami Sakima, the lodge vice-chief or Sakima, the lodge secretary or

LOCAL LODGE BOY OFFICERS

Lodge Chief	Netami Sakima
Lodge Vice-Chief	Sakima
Lodge Secretary	Netami Lekhiket
Lodge Treasurer	Netami Mawachpo

Netami Lekhiket, and the lodge treasurer or Netami Mawachpo. It may be desirable in some bigger lodges to elect more than one vice-chief. Elected officers must be registered in Scouting and in good standing in the lodge. They must be under 21 years of age for their entire term of office. Officers serve for a 1-year term from January 1 through December 31. Officers may be reelected and serve for more than one term. The term coincides with the charter year. Nominations and elections should be held in the fall so that newly elected officers can make a smooth transition into the responsibilities of their offices with the aid of the incumbent officers. All members of the lodge except those who are over 21 are eligible to vote.

Operating committees

If the objectives of an Order of the Arrow lodge in camping promotion and cheerful service are to be reached, it is necessary to organize a number of operating committees.

Committee chairmen are appointed by the lodge chief with the approval of the executive committee, become members of the executive committee, and may pick their own committee members subject to the approval of the lodge chief.

Each operating committee should have one or more adult committee advisers who work closely with the lodge adviser in giving guidance to committee work, and are appointed by the lodge chief in consultation with the lodge and staff adviser.

It is desirable that every Arrowman serve on one or more of the committees. In this way, each member shares the responsibility for lodge activities and projects and lodge officers are not burdened with all the details of meeting lodge objectives.

Here are some of the basic lodge operating committees:

Service committee — suggests a yearly schedule of service projects, gets lodge approval, and makes complete plans for getting the work done. The camping and activities committee representative is usually the committee adviser.

Activities committee — develops plans for three of four membership meeting activities for the lodge each year and is responsible for carrying them out.

Finance committee—draws up an annual budget; issues regular finance reports, obtaining its information from the council office;

supervises the work of the treasurer; and is responsible for the financial status of the lodge.

Unit elections committee—sends out information to unit leaders about elections, organizes and trains election teams, schedules visits of election teams to units, and receives and records the results of elections.

Ceremonial committee — trains ceremonial teams, instructs members on costume making, keeps ceremonial grounds in good order, and conducts ceremonies and demonstrations for the lodge.

Membership committee—checks on inactive members and maintains membership records, sends out letters each year to determine active members and checks address changes, sends letters to Ordeal members eligible for Brotherhood membership, prepares lodge bulletins.

Camping promotion committee— develops plans for camping promotion in consultation with the camping and activities committee; develops promotion helps such as "where to go" camping booklets, visual aids, color slides, and movies of camping activities. It is the adviser's job to provide training and coaching for the committee members.

Certain committees are sometimes appointed on a temporary basis to carry out some specific assignment—a nominating committee, a Vigil Honor committee, a lodge rules committee, or a committee to run a single service project for a banquet or for a major lodge activity.

Some of the bigger lodges broaden their committee structure to include editorial, public relations, Indian dance team, Indian costume committees, etc.

Lodge executive committee

The executive committee of the lodge—a key group—is made up

45

of lodge boy officers (including the past lodge chief), operating committee chairmen, the staff adviser, and the lodge adviser and another member of the camping and activities committee. If it is felt that this group is not representative, a lodge may select two or three members at large—Indian lore or public relations experts, for instance—to serve on the committee. If there are chapters in the lodge, the chapter chiefs and chapter advisers are members of the lodge executive committee. Any lodge member is welcome to attend executive committee meetings as an observer.

The executive committee is the steering committee of the lodge. It faces the problems, studies possible solutions, and then, through the lodge committee organization, acts. It carries on the business of the lodge, coordinating the work being done by officers and operating committees.

The lodge chief is chairman and presides over meetings. He should prepare agenda in advance of meetings and send them to committee members with the meeting announcement.

A definite schedule for executive committee meetings is established before the start of the lodge year. Monthly or once-every-2-months meetings are the customary pattern. Each committee member should have a schedule of the meetings. It is understood that the lodge chief or Scout executive is privileged to call a special meeting of the committee, if the need arises.

The executive committee is a relatively small group and, thus, able to handle the business of the lodge in an efficient manner. The entire membership of the lodge should, however, hear a report of all major decisions and projects being planned and should vote on all major proposals. They need not be burdened by making the decisions on routine business matters.

Those members of the executive committee who are staff members at summer camp may serve as the Arrow camp council to handle Order of the Arrow business during camp. The lodge chief will want to appoint someone to serve in his place as camp chief, if he is not at camp himself.

Annual charter procedure

Each lodge must apply every year to the national office, Boy Scouts of America, for the renewal of its charter. A form is provided for this purpose that must be completed and returned with the information asked for and the charter fee during January of each year. Lodges that fail to renew their charter within this period are lapsed and their orders for supplies, literature, or Vigil Honor petitions are not honored.

Charters may be reinstated at any time by paying the current year's charter fee and supplying the required information about the lodge to the national office.

Membership records

Each lodge must keep accurate membership records at all times. It is often desirable for the lodge to make arrangements with the local council office so that space can be provided in their files for the necessary records. The lodge secretary will, of course, be responsible for maintaining them.

It is suggested that a card file or loose-leaf form be developed and then mimeographed for the lodge secretary to use in keeping membership records. A special Order of the Arrow Record Book, No. 5038, with loose-leaf forms is available from our Supply Division. It was developed at the request of a number of lodges. If a card file is preferred, the card should be similar to the one shown on this page.

ORDER OF THE ARROW MEMBERSHIP RECORD CARD

Name: Thomas J. Jones

Mailing address: 405 Chestnut Street, Boise, Idaho

Home phone: IN 4-3356   Business phone: None

Type unit and number: Explorer Post 41

Candidate's birth date: November 5, 1951

Date of election: October 16, 1963

Date of induction to Ordeal: November 12, 1963

Date of Brotherhood membership ceremony: December 1, 1964

Date of election and induction to Vigil Honor:

Offices and committee memberships held:

Original membership fee paid: November 13, 1963

Record of dues paid each year: $2-1963; $2-1964; $2-1965

An "inactive file" should be kept so that there will always be a record available of the history of past members.

When a member moves and wishes to be transferred to another lodge, the council office should forward a letter stating the details of his active membership in the Order to the Scout executive of the new council. A space is provided for Order of the Arrow record on the regular membership transfer form.

Lodge membership fee and dues

Each lodge sets its own fee for joining and annual dues. Both should be kept to a minimum.

The original fee usually ranges from $2 to $3—enough to cover the cost of the new member's Arrow sash, *Order of the Arrow Handbook,* and Arrow pin which are given to him by the lodge.

Since the expenses of the lodge are generally small it is suggested that the annual dues be within the $1 to $2 bracket. They are customarily paid at the first of each year or at the time of the annual lodge meeting.

Lodge rules should provide for a fixed date by which dues for the coming year must be paid by all active members. Since the charter renewal fee of the lodge is due each year before January 31, December 1 is a sensible date to set as a deadline for payment.

The record of dues paid should be kept in the official lodge records maintained by the lodge secretary. If the lodge treasurer lives in a different community, duplicate records must be kept for the record of dues received and transmitted to the lodge secretary for entry on the official records.

Membership certificates should always be issued promptly upon payment of dues.

Because the Order of the Arrow is an official part of the total program of the Boy Scouts of America, the finances of the lodge should be included in the council treasury and subject to council regulations and auditing procedure. Though the lodge treasurer must maintain a record of those members who are in good standing, the mechanics of maintaining a treasury are the concern of the council.

Forming a new lodge

Inquiries about establishing an Order of the Arrow lodge should be directed to the Camping and Conservation Service of the Boy

Scouts of America. Preliminary information and an application will be sent immediately upon the request of the Scout executive. After thoroughly studying the material and becoming acquainted with the principles and purpose of the Order of the Arrow, the matter should be brought before the camping and activities committee of the local council. Upon receiving the approval of the camping and activities committee, final action must be taken by the council executive board. When this has been done, the lodge charter application is completed and forwarded to the Camping and Conservation Service at the national office together with the charter fee.

Organizing committee. One or two key Scouters in the council may be selected to work with the Scout executive, camp director, and other staff members in setting up initial plans for the organization of the new lodge and selecting the charter members. If there are men in the council who are already members of the Order of the Arrow, they should be asked to participate on this organizing committee.

Members of the organizing committee together with certain council officials, including the council president and the camping and activities chairman, should be invited to become charter members of the lodge.

Selecting charter members. The existing situation in the local council will determine the procedures to be followed by the organizing committee in selecting the charter members. Unless the new lodge is replacing another honor society, it is desirable to have the first boy members elected to membership right in their own units. All unit leaders are sent a letter telling them of the plans being made to organize a lodge, and that all camping units will have an opportunity to elect one or two Scouts or Explorers to charter membership in the new lodge.

If it is practical, a council-wide orientation meeting for unit leaders and others interested may be held.

Later unit leaders conduct elections at a suggested time and report the results to the council office. Wherever possible, an Order member should attend the meeting and assist the unit leader with the election.

If it is not possible to arrange for individual unit elections, a small group of outstanding Scout campers (5 to 15) may be selected by the organizing committee as the charter members of the lodge. This group would work with the organizing committee in arranging for the first unit elections.

Converting local honor groups to Order of the Arrow. In some instances local camping honor groups are working out very well and are using a program similar to the Order of the Arrow. Recognizing the advantages of using the Order of the Arrow program, these local honor groups often simply take their present membership and induct them all as charter members of the new Order of the Arrow lodge. The induction ceremony can usually be arranged through the area leader so that the actual ceremony is conducted by a ceremonial team from some nearby chartered lodge.

Forming lodge chapters

Order of the Arrow lodges vary in membership from about 50 to over 3,000 members. In some lodges a chapter plan is a necessity, if the objectives of the Order are to be realized. In other lodges there are few members and a chapter plan would be of little value. For these reasons, the National Order of the Arrow Committee has purposely left the deci-

sion of forming chapters in the hands of the lodge officers and Scout executives who know their area best.

Before organizing chapters within a lodge the council staff, lodge officers, and advisers should thoroughly study these factors—
• The active membership of the lodge
• The geography of the council
• If each chapter should include one district or several
• If there should be more than one chapter in a given district
• The territory that will comprise the chapter areas
• The potential members and leaders available in the chapter area
• If the advantages of the chapter plan offset the additional job of lodge administration that results
• If the best interests of Scouting will be served through a chapter plan

After a careful study of the above factors, if the Scout executive feels sure that new chapters are needed, he appoints the chapter adviser in consultation with the lodge adviser, lodge chief, district camping and activities chairman, and the lodge staff adviser. This chapter adviser represents the Scout executive at chapter meetings and activities in the same way that the lodge adviser does with the entire lodge. He also becomes a member of the district camping and activities committee in his district.

The chapter staff adviser is usually the district Scout executive who serves the area in which the chapter operates. He works closely with the lodge staff adviser to assure proper coordination of lodge and chapter activities. He also promotes cooperation between the district camping and activities committee and the membership of the chapter.

CHAPTER BOY OFFICERS

Chapter Chief—
 Wajauwe Netame

Chapter Vice-Chief—
 Equiwi Wajauwe

Chapter Secretary—Lekhiket

Chapter Treasurer—Mawachpo

The chapter officers are nominated and elected by the boy members of the chapter in the same way as lodge officers are elected. Their duties are the same on the chapter level as those of lodge officers on the lodge level. The chapter chief and the chapter adviser become members of the lodge executive committee. Each chapter should have the same operating committees as the parent lodge. The chairmen of these committees would then become members of the corresponding lodge operating committee.

When a chapter plan of operation is firmly established, most of the Order of the Arrow projects, ceremonies, and activities can be carried out on a chapter basis. It should be possible for each chapter to train ceremonial teams to conduct the Ordeal and Ordeal ceremonies, as well as the Brotherhood membership ceremony. Vigil Honor ceremonies probably should be left in the hands of lodge officers. Service projects should be cleared with the district camping and activities committees. The year-round program of the chapter must be coordinated with the program of the district and of the lodge.

When bigger lodges operate on an effective chapter basis, each chapter becomes, in many ways, like a small lodge. In this way, many more boys are given an opportunity to demonstrate leadership ability and to share in the responsibility of giving cheerful service to their units and the districts in which they live.

Under a well-established chapter plan, the entire lodge seldom gets together. Each chapter plans its program to carry out the objectives of the lodge. Such events as calling out ceremonies, Ordeals, and Ordeal ceremonies can easily be conducted by chapter personnel. Service projects and social events lend themselves better to smaller groups than the entire lodge. Some chapters develop dance teams, hold father-and-son banquets, camp-outs, and other normal Arrow activities.

When the entire lodge gets together for a fall reunion, an annual meeting or a weekend conclave, the event takes on the atmosphere of an area fellowship conference. This should be an event for fun, fellowship, inspiration, and training.

STANDARD LOCAL COUNCIL LODGE RULES

*These rules may not be changed by the local lodge.

I. Name and affiliation of lodge

A. The name of this lodge of the Order of the Arrow shall be the _____-W. W. W.

*B. The lodge shall be affiliated with _____ Council, Boy Scouts of America and shall be under the supervision of the council camping and activities committee and the administrative authority of the Scout executive.

C. The totem and call of this lodge shall be that of the _____ _____.

D. The standard set of colors for lodge neckerchiefs shall be _____ _____.

1. Each member shall receive only one official lodge neckerchief that is not to be traded or resold.

2. Lodge neckerchiefs and sashes shall be worn only at Order of the Arrow functions.

E. This lodge shall be divided into (number) chapters. Each chapter shall come under the supervision of the related district camping and activities committee(s) and the district Scout executive(s).

II. Election to membership

*A. The requirements for membership in this lodge are as required in the *Order of the Arrow Handbook*.

*B. Procedure for the Ordeal shall be as stated in the *Order of the Arrow Handbook*.

C. All elections must clear through the unit elections committee.

III. Officers

*A. The officers of this lodge shall be lodge chief, lodge vice-chief, lodge secretary, and lodge treasurer. These elected officers must be under 21 years of age for their entire term of office.

B. The officers of each chapter of this lodge shall be chapter chief, vice-chief, treasurer, and secretary. These elected officers must be under 21 years of age for their entire term of office.

C. Lodge officers shall be elected (date and place).
The term of all officers, chapter and lodge, shall be from January 1 to December 31, and they shall be installed (date and event).

*D. The executive committee shall be composed of the four elected lodge officers; the immediate past lodge chief; the lodge operating committee chairman; the lodge adviser; a member of the camping and activities committee; the chapter chief and the adviser to each chapter; the Scout executive and the staff adviser.

*E. The lodge adviser and chapter advisers shall be appointed by the Scout executive in consultation with the related camping and activities committee chairmen.

F. The lodge chief shall appoint such operating committees as may be required from time to time with the approval of the lodge executive committee; all chairmen shall be under 21 years of age.

G. The chapter chief shall appoint such operating committees as may be required from time to time with the approval of the chapter executive committee; all chairmen shall be under 21 years of age.

IV. Lodge meetings

A. The lodge shall schedule lodge events as listed:
    (Examples are optional.)
    1. Fall planning conference
    2. Christmas dinner dance

3. Business meeting

4. Camp service — fellowship weekend

B. The executive committee of this lodge shall hold at least four meetings a year.

C. Special meetings of the executive committee or of the lodge may be called by the lodge chief with the approval of the Scout executive or by the Scout executive.

D. Each meeting of the lodge shall be opened with the Obligation of the Order of the Arrow.

*E. Members of the Order, 21 years of age or over, shall have no vote in any decisions of the lodge.

V. Dues

A. There shall be an induction fee of $____ payable at the time of induction. For such, each new Ordeal member shall receive:

1. An Order of the Arrow pin on red and white ribbon

2. A membership card

3. An Order of the Arrow sash

4. An *Order of the Arrow Handbook.*

B. Dues of the lodge shall be collected annually by the chapter treasurer in the amount of $____, to be given to the lodge treasurer immediately for deposit with the council office. Dues must be paid by December 31.

C. In the development of the lodge annual budget, funds will be made available for chapter mailings, activities, and service projects. Chapters must gain approval from the lodge treasurer and adviser before incurring expenses. All approved bills will be paid by the council office.

*D. All Order of the Arrow funds shall be handled through the council office and go through all normal accounting procedures used by the council.

E. Inactive members may be restored to active status by paying back dues for 1 year and the current dues.

VI. Brotherhood membership

*A. Completion of Brotherhood membership shall be in accordance with the *Order of the Arrow Handbook.*

54

*VII. The Vigil Honor

A. Attainment of the Vigil Honor shall be in accordance with the *Order of the Arrow Handbook*.

VIII. Amendments to rules

A. These rules shall be subject to amendment at any regular or special meeting of this lodge provided such amendment has been submitted in writing to the executive committee at least 1 month prior to such meeting and that due notice has been sent to all active members at least 10 days prior to such meeting. A two-thirds vote of the members present shall be required.

CHAPTER FIVE

COMMUNICATIONS

The very nature of an Order of the Arrow lodge makes communications an important consideration. The lodge or chapters do not meet frequently and all members are not able to attend lodge activities. The vital work of the Brotherhood of cheerful service is done by individual Arrowmen in their own units. Therefore, it is essential that a large measure of the information needed by members be distributed through the mails.

Each lodge should publish a bulletin for all of its members at regular intervals. While monthly bulletins may be necessary for some lodges, other lodges find that a bulletin published every other month or every third month will do the job.

A lodge bulletin should carry such essential information to the member as announcements and promotional stories of forthcoming lodge and chapter events, news of interest about lodge members and their activities, inspirational stories, letters to the editor, and editorials.

Some bulletins devote a small section to news from each chapter written by a chapter correspondent. Others include features on Indian costume making, Indian dancing, and Indian customs.

Jokes, poems, and cartoons can help hold the interest of the readers. Certainly stories about area fellowship meetings, training events, and national Order of the Arrow news should have a place in every lodge bulletin.

It is not necessary that each chapter publish a regular bulletin. Chapter information can be carried in the lodge bulletin. Some chapters may find it desirable to publish a newsletter from time to time, but generally the essential communications can be adequately covered in the regular lodge bulletin.

In making up a bulletin — whether it's mimeographed or printed — here are some tips:

Don't crowd your pages with print. Leave air space between headings on a page. This will improve the appearance of your bulletin and make it easier to read.

Narrow columns, about newspaper width, are less tiring for a reader than 4- or 5-inch columns.

Test your stories and announcements to see if they answer the questions *who, what, when, why,* and *where.* For instance, to say that a meeting will be held on Friday the 14th doesn't fully answer the question *when* because the time of day, month, and year are missing.

Another general rule in bulletin writing is to keep words and sentences short. Five-syllable words and 70-word sentences irk and slow down most readers.

Our national bulletin

An *Order of the Arrow Bulletin* is published quarterly in the national office in New Brunswick, N. J., and copies are mailed to each lodge chief in care of the local council office. There are normally enough for lodge officers, advisers, and related staff members without any charge to the local lodge for this service. Any Order member may, if he wishes, subscribe to the *Order of the Arrow Bulletin* at the rate of 40 cents a year. It will then be mailed to his home.

News items of national interest may be sent to the national secretary, who is editor of the bulletin. Success stories and photographs about local lodge activities are always welcome.

It is a good plan for each local council office to have arrangements made to hold or forward mail from the national office directed to the lodge chief.

CHAPTER SIX

TRAINING OPPORTUNITIES

61

If Order of the Arrow lodges are to continue to be successful, it is necessary that lodge officers and advisers be trained to know their jobs. Since the membership of the Order is undergoing continual change, with new members being inducted and older members graduating from the ranks, there should be a planned training program in each lodge.

The purpose of this training program is to acquaint every lodge officer and committee chairman with the complete scope of his job. Each officer must understand the high purpose of the lodge and how each officer can contribute to the success of the lodge through his own leadership and program of action.

A firm objective of this training is to ensure the lodge and its membership a year of action and accomplishment. A prerequisite to all this is well-informed lodge leadership.

A further objective is to establish correct and effective patterns of lodge operation, conforming to the very best traditions of the Order of the Arrow and the standards approved by the national committee.

The training conference should be held in the fall. Election of officers for most lodges takes place at the fall business meeting each year. The lodge charter year is from January 1 to December 31. If new officers are elected in September or October, then the retiring officers can help train their successors before they take office at the first of the year. This overlap system works well in many lodges. Lodges may arrange to conduct training conferences to suit their own needs. It is well to bring the council leadership training and camping committees into plans for training.

Those who should attend the conference are the lodge chief, vice-chiefs, secretary, treasurer, lay advisers, staff advisers, chapter chiefs, all chapter officers, all committee chairmen, and all members at large of the lodge executive committee.

The best place to conduct the training is the council camp. Some councils have training centers that would be most suitable. Other lodges may wish to hold the training meeting in town at a school, the Y.M.C.A., or a hotel. The place where training is conducted should have a Scoutlike atmosphere.

The time needed to conduct the training conference is 8 hours. Following is the complete training course with references to this *Order of the Arrow Handbook.*

LODGE OFFICERS' TRAINING CONFERENCE

FRIDAY

Dinner at 6:30 p.m.—Keynote talk	15 min.
Session One—7:30 to 9:30 p.m.	2 hrs.
Cracker Barrel—9:30 to 10:00 p.m.	

SATURDAY

Breakfast at 7:30 a.m.—Big idea	15 min.
Session Two—9.00 to 10:15 a.m.	1 hr. 15 min.
Break—10:15 to 10:30 a.m.	
Session Three—10:30 to 11:45 a.m.	1 hr. 15 min.
Luncheon at 12:00 noon	
Session Four—1:00 to 2:15 p.m.	1 hr. 15 min.
Break—2:15 to 2:30 p.m.	
Final session—2:30 to 3:30 p.m.	1 hr.

Responsibility for conducting the training conference rests with the lodge advisers, but the lodge chief may wish to appoint a special committee to make the necessary arrangements.

Materials needed

- *Order of the Arrow Handbook* for each member

- *The Order of the Arrow (The Symbol of Service)* filmstrip and recording available from the Audiovisual Service, Boy Scouts of America, New Brunswick, N.J. 08903. Price $12.25.

- Filmstrip projector, record player, and screen

- Note paper and pencils

Opening session

Dinner or general assembly of the group

Fifteen-minute talk on the purpose of the Order of the Arrow. (The Supreme Chief of the Fire, the Scout executive of the local council, is the most logical one to make this presentation.) He should emphasize purpose of the Order, page 5, *Order of the Arrow Handbook*.

Session one (2 hrs.)

Order of the Arrow filmstrip and handbook review:

1. Opening ceremony

a. Pledge to the flag.

b. Repeat the Scout Oath.

c. Repeat Order of the Arrow Obligation (printed on back of official membership card).

2. Introduction of filmstrip. Ask each member to be prepared to note questions that arise as the filmstrip is being shown. These will be answered by a panel after showing of the strip. All questions must pertain to the filmstrip material.

3. Show filmstrip *The Order of the Arrow (The Symbol of Service)* with recording.

4. Discuss filmstrip presentation. A panel of three members, including the lodge adviser, should be prepared to conduct this session. Instructor asks each member to stand and read his question; then asks some one in the group to answer it. If an answer is not forthcoming from the trainees, a member of the panel answers the question. If a satisfactory answer is not given, the instructor appoints one or two members of the group to find the answer in the *Order of the Arrow Handbook* or other source, and report later.

5. Review the *Order of the Arrow Handbook*. (Each member should have a handbook in his hands.) This 30-minute session could be handled by an Arrowman in the form of a book review by quickly going through the book, pointing out the main headings, and showing how to find answers to questions as they arise.

It is highly recommended that every member be given a copy of the handbook at the time of his induction and asked to read it when he first becomes a member.

6. Closing
Inspirational minute—A Scout Is Helpful.
Cracker barrel
Taps
Breakfast. A 10- to 15-minute in-

spirational big idea. This talk should be on the spiritual motivation of the Order—the theme of cheerful service, of setting a good example for our fellow Scouts and Explorers, or of living up to the ideals of the Scout Oath and Law. It is suggested that this talk be given by a boy, giving him plenty of time for advance preparation. An adviser could be appointed to help the young man develop a fine inspirational message that will set the stage for the day.

Session two (1 hr. 15 min.)

Lodge organization and administration:

1. Position of the Scout executive

OAHB — page 40; page 11, The Order and the local council; page 40, Lodge adult advisers; page 43, Local lodge boy officers; page 53, Section III, A-G, Officers; page 22, Executive (ex officio) membership

2. The lodge adviser and the staff adviser

OAHB — page 41, Lodge adviser's role in the Order; page 42, Staff adviser's role in the Order; page 40, Adult role in the Order

3. Local lodge boy officers

OAHB — page 43; page 24, Ordeal master's job

4. Lodge executive committee

OAHB—page 45; page 53, Section III, D; page 54, Section IV, B, C

5. Committee organization and responsibilities

OAHB—page 53, Section III, F, G; page 44, Operating committees

6. Standard local council lodge rules.

OAHB—pages 52-55

7. Finances

OAHB—page 48, lodge membership fee and dues; page 54, Section V, A-E, Dues

8. Membership records

OAHB—page 47

9. Forming lodge chapters

OAHB—pages 50-52; page 52, Section I, E; page 53, Section III, G

Break

Session three (1 hr. 15 min.)

Planning for a year-round balanced program:

OAHB—pages 80-85. The prime purpose of activities or program is to give focus to the aims, purposes, and objectives of the lodge so that objectives can be attained.

1. Basic principles

a. An Arrowman's first responsibility is to his unit. No Order of the Arrow program or activity should tend to take a boy away from his own unit.

b. Cheerful service to others is the cornerstone of the Order, therefore, a balanced program will include opportunities for service.

c. The promotion of Scout camping is another primary objective of the Order of the Arrow. Every lodge should include camping promotion as a major project of its entire membership.

d. The opportunity for fellowship and fun should be planned into the program. The Order of the Arrow is the "brotherhood of cheerful service." Put the accent on cheerfulness and brotherhood.

2. Types of activities

a. Lodge meetings—fellowship, elections, training (the number of meetings of the entire membership should be reduced to a minimum by working through committees).

b. Chapter meetings—as above

c. Ceremonial meetings—calling out, Ordeal, and Brotherhood

d. Service projects—camp work periods, camping promotion, publication of "where to go" camping booklets, etc.

e. Social activities — fellowship lodge meetings, father-and-son dinner, sponsorship of an Explorer dance, etc.

f. Lodge projects—making costumes, building ceremonial teams, developing dance teams, etc.

3. Special care should be taken to coordinate plans for Order of the Arrow activity with the calendar for district and council events. All plans pertaining to camping promotion and service to the camping program should be carefully checked with the council camping and activities committee. Promotion plans in

each district must be made in co-operation with the district camping and activities committee. The lodge should then publish an activities calendar showing date and time and place of all Order of the Arrow meetings, ceremonies, and service projects.

4. It would be well to use a developmental discussion at this point. List all ideas from the group on program and activities on a blackboard or large sheet of paper. Get as many suggestions from trainees as time will allow. Then by discussing items in light of the previous presentation, determine the most practical year-round program for the lodge. The suggestions of the group could very well become the basic plan for the lodge during the next year. Refer to the filmstrip presentation as it relates to program. Use the handbook as a reference.

Luncheon

Session four (1 hr. 15 min.)

Interpreting national standards and policies:
This session concerns self-examination of your own lodge with such questions as: How effective is our lodge? Are we meeting our responsibilities and obligations? Are we operating according to national standards?

If your lodge can answer all of the 16 questions affirmatively, then it is a topflight lodge. If there are some negative answers, then the officers should find ways to bring the lodge up to this high standard. The questions could be written on a blackboard or large sheet of paper or duplicated in advance and given to each Arrowman.

There will probably be shades of "yes" and "no" in some of the answers. Discuss each question and rate it according to how effective your lodge is—excellent, good, fair, or poor. Then discuss ways of making the lodge more effective.

1. Are staff advisers and lodge advisers actively participating in lodge affairs?

2. Are the chief and officers of the lodge trained for their responsibilities?

3. Are elections for new candidates held every year in each unit eligible to hold elections?

4. Are all candidates called out at an impressive public ceremony in a Scout camping atmosphere?

5. Are Ordeals and induction ceremonies conducted according to national standards?

a. Do ceremonial teams know their parts?

b. Are proper costumes worn by the team?

c. Do Ordeal work projects really contribute to the improvement of camping facilities?

6. Does the lodge have a balanced year-round program including:

a. Ceremonials with fellowship opportunities?

b. Worthwhile service projects in connection with camp improvement and development?

c. A well-planned camping promotion program?

d. Opportunities for the entire membership to participate in the lodge program?

7. Is there an annual lodge written program with dates set in advance?

8. Does the lodge participate in the annual area fellowship conference?

9. Is the administration of the lodge set up on a committee basis with every member assigned to a specific committee?

10. Does the executive committee meet on a regular schedule?

11. Is a lodge bulletin published at least every 3 months?

12. If chapter plan is used, do all chapters operate effectively?

13. Is a Brotherhood membership ceremony held at least once each year, and are those eligible invited to seal their membership through the Brotherhood ceremony?

14. Is a Vigil Honor call out and ceremony conducted at least once each year and carried out according to prescribed methods?

15. Are all Order of the Arrow members active in their own units and registered as members of the Boy Scouts of America?

16. Does the lodge conduct its financial affairs on a businesslike basis, and are funds handled through the council office?

Break

1. Brief review in the *OAHB* of the requirements for Boy membership, page 16; Scouter elections, page 17; Ordeal membership, pages 22-29; Brotherhood membership, pages 29-32; The Vigil Honor, pages 32-36; (Members should follow along in their *Order of the Arrow Handbook*.)

2. Summing it up (a 15-minute review by an adviser covering the findings of the session). He should be prepared to point out the areas in which the lodge is doing very well and mention the areas where some improvement needs to be made. He can make specific recommendations at this point. He should wind up with a challenge to do our best to live up to the high ideals of the Scout Oath and Law and to exemplify the Order of the Arrow's spirit of cheerful service in our daily lives.

3. Closing ceremony. Form the fellowship circle, joining hands right over left, and sing "The Order of the Arrow Official Song."

AREA FELLOWSHIP TRAINING CONFERENCE

The area fellowship training conference presents a splendid opportunity for learning more about the Order.

Lodges in each area should gather for an area fellowship training meeting annually or biennially. Area meetings are held for the purpose of—
- Creating good fellowship
- Developing interest and enthusiasm
- Providing for the sharing of new methods or ideas
- Promoting workable procedures for effective local lodge operation
- Providing opportunities for young man leadership and participation

The area leader advises and works with the area conference chief in planning and conducting the area conference.

Preconference planning — The area leader and area adviser request that capable young men, usually lodge officers, representing each lodge in the area, attend a special planning session several months before the area meeting is to be held. At this preliminary conference, the general program is planned and necessary arrangements made. Responsibilities are delegated so that every lodge in the area may participate in preparing for the meeting. The area conference chief works side by side with the area leader and area adviser in directing the planning. The regional adviser should be invited to participate in this planning session.

Promotion — After the regional office and the Scout executives of the area have approved the dates of the meeting, the area leader and adviser supervise the promotion of the area meeting through advance publicity to local lodges. Colorful newsletters, bulletins, and invitations can often reflect the very flavor of the meeting right from the start. Emphasis in promotional literature is placed upon the importance of having every lodge represented at the meeting.

Fees—The individual registration fee for an area meeting should be set upon the recommendation of the host lodge and the general agreement of the other lodges in the area. Fees should be high enough to cover all of the expenses involved in the meeting, but they should not be set with the idea of making a profit on the

meeting. They should be kept within reason so that as many members as possible will be able to attend. Surplus funds, after paying expenses, can be returned to participating lodges on a pro rata basis or held in trust to be used for the next conference.

Host lodge—Members of the host lodge for the area meeting begin to work well ahead of time in making the physical arrangements. They need to provide the best possible meals, adequate arrangements for sleeping, and necessary facilities to carry out the conference program. The host lodge makes the preparations for religious services, a first aid station, a corps of guides, a trading post or canteen, etc. The host lodge should not be saddled with the additional responsibility of planning and executing the program. Program is the responsibility of the area leader, area adviser, and area conference chief who call on other lodges to participate.

Registration—A swift moving efficient method of registration creates a good first impression. At this time those attending the meeting may be provided with a printed program of events and individual name cards to wear on their uniforms during the meeting.

Report—As soon as possible following the conference, a well-written report describing the highlights of the meeting and presenting the summaries of discussion sessions should be distributed to the brothers attending the meeting. Some areas have this report mimeographed and ready for distribution to the group at the closing session of the area meeting. A copy of the report should be sent to the regional office and to the national secretary.

Fellowship training conference program suggestions

Inspiration—It is important that the meeting gets off to a good start with a warm welcome from the host lodge and some short but significant ceremony or address which will set the tone for the entire conference. It is equally important that the meeting close with an inspirational challenge that will create a lasting impression for every member. At other times throughout the meeting, young men may be called upon for keynote speeches or for first-hand reports of jamborees and national conferences.

Demonstrations — Several different lodges may easily participate in various demonstrations that will be of value to those attending. These might include:

The three Arrow ceremonies performed by well-rehearsed teams.

Unique and significant calling out ceremonies.

An interview with the candidates during their Ordeal.

A well-planned campfire.

Indian or Scouting pageants.

A parade or demonstration of Indian regalia.

Indian dancing.

Discussions — Area meetings should provide an opportunity for the brothers to get together in smaller groups for periods of discussion. It is well to choose able young Order of the Arrow leaders as discussion group leaders and designate older members with more years of experience to serve as advisers for each group. The discussion leader should be informed of his responsibility in sufficient time to make careful preparation. It has been found successful to have the leader present a brief talk on the topic before the actual discussion begins. A recorder should be appointed to take notes on the discussion. Suggested topics are:

LODGE ADMINISTRATION—Relationship of adult advisers to young men officers, responsibilities of officers and advisers, standing committees, operation of lodge executive committee, general policies, lodge rules, election procedures, chapter organization, and programs.

LODGE ACTIVITIES – Importance of well-balanced, well-planned yearly program, social activities, annual banquets. Specific ideas for events and scheduling on the council calendar.

ARROW-SCOUTING RELATIONSHIP—Arrowman and the unit, Arrow and the camp, authority of Scout executive, relationships with Scout council and the camping and activities committee.

SERVICE PROJECTS—Promotion of year-round camping, service to local units, council-wide projects, service to the camp, and coordination of service program with camping and activities committee plans.

CEREMONIES – Training of teams, costuming, staging, physical setting, timing, properties, calling out ceremonies.

CONDUCTING THE ORDEAL—Spirit of the Ordeal, duties of Ordeal master, relationship of candidates to campers, discussion period for candidates, health safeguards, and handling flagrant violations.

LODGE PUBLICATIONS—Bulletins, newsletters, yearbooks, costs involved, frequency, distribution.

BROTHERHOOD MEMBERSHIP—Purpose, qualifications, procedures, informing Ordeal members, questioning period, place of Brotherhood members in the lodge.

LODGE RECORDS – Membership, financial, minutes, registration procedures, lodge record book available from the Supply Division of the Boy Scouts of America.

VIGIL HONOR – Qualifications, procedures, relationship of these members to the lodge.

ALPHA PHI OMEGA—An explanation of what it is, purpose and program. Full information available from the Order of the Arrow national secretary or from the national Alpha Phi Omega office, 1100 Waltower Building, 823 Walnut Street, Kansas City, Mo. 64106.

Skill instruction—A special period is often set aside for workshop or skill groups on various phases of Indian lore. Usually these sessions are most successful if they are aimed at providing basic information rather than highly technical skills and knowledge. Skill sessions might be held on any of the following:

Indian dancing
Making costumes
Headdress construction
Beadwork
Ceremonial properties

Displays—At some central spot, various displays may be arranged such as those mentioned below. Each lodge should prepare its own exhibit of lodge bulletins and pictures of its activities, and the best display given a prize.

Local lodge publications
Pictures of lodge events and service projects
Ceremonial regalia
Indian costume and headdress kits available from the Supply Division of the Boy Scouts of America
Order of the Arrow literature and supplies
Local lodge emblems
Interesting items of Indian lore and camping gear that are available locally
Indian Lore merit badge pamphlet

Recreation—Variety and spark can be added to the program by arranging for recreational activities such as the following:

Sports events with lodge competition
Field meets
Games and stunts that test camping skills

Hikes and tours of the camp
Water carnivals or swimming meets
Boating and canoeing
Movies or slides on camping, Indian lore or outdoor life
Camp-wide games
Archery and riflery contests
Industrial and historical expeditions
Campfires
Nature and woodlore activities

Fellowship—Some areas appoint a special committee to plan events that will encourage good fellowship and high morale. Here are some that have worked well:

Select capable young song leaders to direct songfests after meals or later in the evening.

Try some type of contest that lasts over the entire period of the conference such as the best individually carved cane, totem, arrow, or neckerchief slide or have the members search for various hidden articles around the camp.

Plan a fellowship campfire and pull together the very best talent available for a big "pow wow" or "whooperoo."

Designate a different young member to preside at each meal, arrange for the grace, obtain song leaders, and make announcements.

Arrange for late evening snacks as they always make a big hit.

Schedule a little free time for the group. Exchanging ideas at bull sessions is a major event at area meetings.

Arrange for an outdoor barbecue in place of one of the meals in the dining hall.

Have the host lodge plan to present to all members attending the area meeting some sort of memento such as an emblem, neckerchief slide, or banner.

Other features—Toward the close of the meeting, the area leader and conference chief may want to hold a business meeting of the entire membership to discuss such plans for the future as election of a new area conference chief, selection of the host lodge for the next area meeting, and the dates for this meeting. At this time a report of the attendance at the area meeting may be presented and a special award or recognition given to the lodge with the biggest attendance, the greatest number of "man-miles" traveled, or the greatest percentage of active lodge membership attending.

The area leader may wish to arrange for a special session with Scout executives and lodge advisers to discuss common points of interest.

Another type session might be a question-and-answer period or an open forum at which the members may direct specific questions to a group of experienced leaders in the area.

Sample program outline—Here is the outline of a typical program for an area fellowship training meeting. It is not necessarily intended that this particular program be followed by the areas, because one of the significant features about these conferences is their individuality in the different areas of the country and the variations that are made in area meeting programs from year to year. This sample program, however, will be particularly helpful as a working guide for new areas and area leaders. Those using it can incorporate into it as many of the ideas given on the previous pages as they wish.

National training courses

National training courses for key officers, members, and advisers are held from time to time in each of the 12 regions. These courses are conducted under the

SAMPLE AREA FELLOWSHIP MEETING OUTLINE

FRIDAY
2:00 Registration, assignment to quarters
Get acquainted, tour of the camp, displays
5:30 Colors
Calling out ceremony for the Ordeal
6:00 Supper
7:00 Recreation
8:30 Opening meeting—fellowship campfire
10:00 Pre-Ordeal ceremony
10:45 Vigil Honor ceremony
11:00 Songfest, snack, fellowship

SATURDAY
8:00 Breakfast
9:30 Discussion groups
11:00 Open forum
12:30 Lunch
2:00 Skill instruction groups
4:00 Swimming meet
5:30 Colors
Calling out ceremony for Brotherhood
6:00 Dinner
7:30 Indian dancing
Indian dramatization
9:00 Brotherhood ceremony
10:00 Ordeal ceremony
11:30 Snack and fellowship

SUNDAY
8:00 Breakfast
9:30 Religious services
11:00 Area business meeting
12:30 Closing dinner
Final challenge
Closing ceremony

direction of the national secretary and the National Order of the Arrow Committee. Their purpose is to train local lodge officers in effective lodge administration, lodge program activities, and service projects with special emphasis on how the lodge supports the year-round camping program in the council, district, and the unit. The training course also serves to interpret and promote better understanding and use of Order of the Arrow policies. It helps to develop standard procedures for Order relationships with regional and national emphasis.

National training courses are usually held in a Scout camp and arrangements are made by mutual agreement of the regional office and the Volunteer Training Service and Camping and Conservation Service.

National Order of the Arrow conference

It has become a tradition of the Order of the Arrow to have national conferences at 2-year intervals. These conferences are usually held on the campus of a major university during the last part of August. It is highly desirable to have every lodge send representatives to these national meetings of Arrowmen from all parts of the country.

The national conference is planned and conducted by the area conference chiefs with the help and guidance of the National Order of the Arrow Committee. Since there are about 70 areas in the country it would make a very large working committee if all area chiefs attended. Therefore, one-half of the chiefs are invited to help plan each national conference, 6 to 8 months in advance of the conference date. The remaining conference chiefs form the planning committee for the next national conference.

Area conference chiefs attending this planning session elect from their number a member who serves as the national conference chief—the highest position that an Arrow member can attain. As such he becomes chairman of the national conference and is responsible for the proper planning and leadership of it.

The conference is held for 4 or 5 days and from 2,500 to 4,000 Arrowmen participate in the discussion groups, training sessions, and fellowship activities. It is a great opportunity for the exchange of ideas, and for meeting with outstanding young Arrowmen from all the States of the Union as well as from some overseas lodges.

Ceremonies, pageants, and demonstrations are presented by the boys themselves. Outstanding speakers are chosen to inspire and inform the many delegates.

It is during the national conferences that the Order of the Arrow Distinguished Service Awards are presented. One day you may attend a conference.

NATIONAL ORDER OF THE ARROW CONFERENCES

1948	Indiana University	G. Kellock Hale, national chairman
1950	Indiana University	J. Richard Wilson, national conference chief
1952	Miami University, Ohio	James R. Montgomery, national conference chief
1954	University of Wyoming	James R. Feil, national conference chief
1956	Indiana University	James L. Waters, national conference chief
1958	University of Kansas	James W. Kolka, national conference chief
1961	Indiana University	Ronald J. Temple, national conference chief
1963	University of Illinois	Robert B. Ellsperman, national conference chief
1965	Indiana University	Michael S. Costello, national conference chief
1967	University of Nebraska	Robert F. Szczys, national conference chief

Throughout the year it is the practice of lodges to confine their activities primarily to those things that have to do with camping. It is most desirable to have lodge activities in camp and certainly in the outdoors. (An exception might be an annual meeting fellowship banquet or a formal business session.)

Some lodges have found it desirable to have a social activity to which they invite their friends. These functions often serve as a means of securing funds for lodge purposes, for providing camp scholarships for underprivileged boys, and for other worthwhile projects. Some activities that have been successfully tried have been hay rides, wiener roasts, fish fries, annual banquets, winter carnivals, canoe trips, roller skating parties, picnics, father-and-son banquets, barbecues, and winter camp-outs.

During the summer season, the lodge program is carried forward in the camp by the Ordeal master, summer camp chief, and the camp director. It usually includes a meeting, early in each camp period, of all members of the Order then in camp, at which time activities in the camp requiring the attention of the lodge are discussed. A summer camp chief should be appointed to give leadership to Arrow affairs in camp. The lodge may also be active (subject to the approval of the camp director) in various phases of the camping program having to do with ceremonies, pageantry, campfires, or in those activities that concern the induction of new members. Indian pageants, other than the dramatization of the legend of the Lenni Lenape, should be presented to groups of campers. The legend should be reserved for lodge and area meetings.

Business meetings are of several types: The executive committee of the lodge should meet monthly or quarterly, depending on the size of the lodge and the scope of its program. Special committee meetings are called as needed by the committee chairman or the committee adviser. General lodge business meetings are usually held quarterly or semiannually at a time when a majority of lodge members can attend.

At the spring and summer meetings, there may be service projects that can be undertaken by the new candidates and older members alike. All members, not only those taking the Ordeal, should work on the service projects.

Calendar of events

Each lodge should develop a calendar of lodge events made up at the fall planning meeting to extend over the following 12, 16, or even 18 months. In arranging the calendar, the other activities of the districts and the council must be considered. School and community activities as well as special religious holidays should be taken into account to avoid conflicts. In devising the calendar, dates of meetings, location, time, and costs enter into the planning procedure. The annual program is then published so that all members can plan to take part. A lodge should avoid planning a program that is too ambitious. A small program that is carried out effectively is far superior to a large mediocre one.

Promoting activities

The finest way to promote lodge activities is to make every event a success. Other effective ways of getting solid participation are by proper coverage in the lodge bulletin, publication and general distribution of the lodge calendar, and postcard and phone-call reminders shortly before the activity. At each event, take time to encourage the members to attend the next scheduled activity.

Rendering services

The main line of the Order of the Arrow program should be directed toward camping promotion, cheerful service to camping, and cheerful service to others. Putting together "where to go" camping booklets for unit leaders, making camping promotion visits to all Scout and Explorer units, carrying on service projects to improve summer camps, and setting high standards of personal conduct are the objectives that every lodge should plan into its program.

To the person inquiring about the Order of the Arrow and reading this handbook for the first time, the question may occur, "Why all of this?" The answer is that the Order functions so that Scouts and Explorers may experience in their lives that kind of motivating force that urges them to service. The following are just a few examples of services that have been rendered by Arrowmen on behalf of Scouting across the country:

Developed, printed, and distributed "where to go" camping booklets for council units.

Spring—Camp service weekend in which service projects are performed for the council camp. Ceremonies can be held, followed by a short business meeting and fellowship activity.

Summer — Completion of a major service project at camp. Ordeal, Brotherhood, and Vigil Honor ceremonies, followed by orientation of new members and short fellowship event, campfire, or barbecue.

ORDER OF THE ARROW

Fall—Annual meeting and yearly planning session to develop the entire year's program, elect new officers, form lodge committees, conduct ceremonies, orient new members, and join in some inspirational fellowship activities.

Winter—Annual banquet (possibly father and son), formal installation of new officers, brief business meeting following the banquet. Other suggestions—A winter carnival at camp, a social event, snowbird hike, skating party, skiing party, or special camping trip.

Conducted camp attendance campaigns

Carried out reforestation programs at the council camp

Developed a cheerful service award for boys at camp

Constructed Adirondack cabins at the summer camp

Eradicated white pine weevil from a white pine forest

Built a camp chapel entrance

Sponsored such council-wide activities as a patrol leaders' conferences, camporees, pre-camp rallies, swimming meets, archery meets, winter camps, and fair exhibits

Prepared instructions on Indian costume making

Built a camp road and stone altar, enclosed campgrounds with a rustic fence, built a cabin out of old railroad ties

Repaired toys, made tepees, improved paths, built nature trails, made camp movies

Values to local councils

A survey conducted by the national office of the Boy Scouts of America among Scout executives having lodges indicated that they place a high value on the Order of the Arrow. Here are some things they mentioned that Arrowmen have done for Scouting:

Aided in developing a deeper and more widespread interest in the outdoor program of Scouting

Inspired and stimulated all campers, members and non-members alike, to become better Scouts and to conduct themselves in such a manner as to merit membership in the Order

Acted as a potent influence in character development

Helped to hold the interest of older boys, build leadership, and thus helped supply junior and eventually senior leaders for troops

Helped Scouts to a better understanding of, and a firmer belief in, the value of cheerful service and unselfish service to others and aided in developing leadership in such service

84

Created and maintained a high morale at camp

Stimulated members and candidates, as well as groups of other campers led by Order members, to do much repair and construction work at camp

Aided the program of Scouting for young men throughout the year by sponsoring social functions, giving leadership to projects of service to others, and helping to promote year-round camping

Helped to make the ideal of the daily Good Turn a reality

Provided experience in democratic procedure through participation in the election of members

I expect to pass this way but once. If, therefore, there be any kindness I can show, or any good thing I can do to any fellow being, let me do it now and not defer or neglect it, as I shall not pass this way again.

William Penn

CHAPTER EIGHT
CEREMONIES

It should be commonly understood that the ceremonies of the Order are set up as a means of dramatizing its high purpose and not as any attempt to imitate the procedures of adult fraternal bodies. The following principles apply:

• The Order of the Arrow is not a secret organization. Its ceremonies therefore, are open to any parent, Scout leader, or religious leader. In its ceremonies it employs the element of mystery for the sake of its effect on the Scouts who enter. Its ceremonies are not put on in public at a camp because this would decrease their appeal to the boy as he first participates. This is the same principle that applies in the Tenderfoot investiture ceremony in many Scout troops.

• The ceremonies used in the Order have been scrutinized to make certain that they are not objectionable to any religious group because of any seeming similarity to religious rites or rituals. Every attempt has been made and always will be made to keep the ceremonies true to Scout tradition and within the spirit of the Scout Oath and Law.

• While the Indian tradition is used in the ceremonies of the Order and in the terminology for the dramatic effect, it is agreed that under no circumstances shall emphasis be placed upon the Indian aspects of the program to the degree that they obscure the objectives of the Order of the Arrow.

Ceremonies are an important part of Order of the Arrow activities and should always be conducted in a manner that is in harmony with the national policy and spirit of the Order.

There is no official calling out ceremony for Ordeal membership, Brotherhood membership, or Vigil Honor. This public recognition has purposely been left in the hands of each lodge. Special pamphlets have been printed containing instructions for conducting the Ordeal, the Ordeal ceremony, the Brotherhood ceremony, and Vigil Honor ceremony. These ceremony pamphlets may be obtained from the Supply Division through the local council office.

Each lodge is encouraged to develop its own calling out ceremony. Here are some principles that should be considered in planning and conducting such a ceremony.

The name and unit number of each candidate should be clearly announced.

The candidates and the audience of boys, parents, and leaders should be made aware of the importance of the honor extended.

Rough stuff, hazing, or any other activity that endangers the health or hurts the feelings of the candidates have no place in any Order of the Arrow ceremony.

The ceremonies should be dramatic, held in the proper setting with full use of Indian costumes, tom-toms, council fires, and Indian dancing if it does not detract from the serious purpose of honoring new candidates.

The calling out ceremonies are to be held in public, at an evening parade, in the dining hall, in the campfire area, or other suitable place.

Those conducting the ceremony should rehearse in advance to avoid slipups and all members should memorize their parts.

One of the most important responsibilities of the lodge officers and advisers is to make sure that the ceremonies of the Order fulfill their high purpose. Lasting impressions that make the difference between success and failure

of an Order of the Arrow lodge start with the ceremonies of the Order. Proper costuming, well-laid-out ceremonial grounds, rehearsals, and memorizing of parts

CEREMONIAL TEAM'S CHECKLIST

Do the Scout executive and camp director know exactly what is planned?

When and where will the ceremony be held?

Who is responsible?

How much time is available?

What is the nature of the ceremony to be?

What costumes are needed?

Are scripts prepared and all parts memorized in advance?

Is the ceremonial area cleaned up and all properties in their place?

Is there any danger to candidates, ceremonial team, or audience?

Will the ceremony impress all who view it with the purpose and solemnity of the occasion?

Is the ceremony in full accord with the principles of the Scout Oath and Law?

all contribute toward successful ceremonies.

Ceremonial grounds

The ceremonies of the Order of the Arrow are among the most beautiful and colorful of any organization. They lend themselves naturally to their outdoor setting and local conditions. Let us not forget though that their success or failure depends on the fundamental rules of good showmanship. In other words, we take up where nature leaves off; and, from there on, the show relies on the properties we use to supplement the natural setting and the organization we set up to ensure proper timing and functioning. These ceremonies and their preparation take time and thought by members of the lodge responsible for the presentation. It is best that a competent chairman with a full committee have charge, and that each of his men be responsible for a certain part of the work to be done.

Choosing ceremonial site

Choosing the site for the ceremony is very important. The more the setting lends itself to the purpose of the ceremony, the more successful your efforts will be to impress the candidates with the beauty and seriousness of the ceremony. The primary things one must keep in mind are privacy, naturalness, and adaptability to the functioning of the ceremonial team. Remember that the ceremonial ring is a project of the whole lodge and the members enjoy the chance to work in building it up, improving it, and making alterations on it during the years. It is a living growing thing,

on which many pleasant hours can be spent by the members.

The physical properties that are to be installed depend entirely on the local situation. As a rule, the minimum requirements are an altar, places for the required number of fires, and a device to hold the candles used in the ceremony. They should blend naturally into the setting so that there is no sharp contrast in the effect as a whole.

The national committee does not prescribe any special proper-ties for the calling out ceremony, but leaves the local lodge to work out an impressive ceremony. Here again is your chance to use your ingenuity to put on an impressive and dignified ceremony, using plenty of color and pageantry. The basic thought or scheme should be based on traditional Indian-lore practices. Here is where you use your tepees, coun-cil fires, and Indians galore. This is your big show—make it a good one that the candidates and audi-ence will remember.

In addition to service, fellowship, and fun during the years of membership in the Order of the Arrow, there are many opportunities for service that Arrowmen can look forward to in the future. The lessons learned in Boy Scouting, Exploring, and in the Order are of great value as the young men of today prepare for positions of leadership tomorrow. Cheerful service to our fellowmen often becomes a lifelong habit. As members of the lodge mature and take their place in adult society, they seek ways and means of continuing their interests in Scouting and service to others.

Alpha Phi Omega

Alpha Phi Omega is a national service fraternity composed of college and university men who are or have been affiliated with the Boy Scouts of America. The purpose of the fraternity is to assemble college men in the fellowship of the Scout Oath and Law, develop friendship, and promote service to humanity.

Service is rendered to the student body and faculty, to youth and the community, and to members of the fraternity and the Nation. Those college students who have had previous training in Scouting, desire to render service to others, and have satisfactory scholastic standing are eligible to apply for membership. Alpha Phi Omega is approved by the Boy Scouts of America. The fraternity is self-governing and self-supporting. It was founded in 1925 at Lafayette College in Easton, Pa., on the banks of the Delaware River. There are over 250 chapters operating on major college and university campuses throughout the country.

Order of the Arrow members who continue their education are urged to seek membership in Alpha Phi Omega. If they attend a college where the fraternity is not established, they can render a great service by helping to organize a chapter. Information can be obtained by writing to the national Alpha Phi Omega office, 1100 Waltower Building, 823 Walnut Street, Kansas City, Mo. 64106.

College Scouter Reserve

For an annual fee of $1, college students can keep up their registered status in the Boy Scouts of America and remain active in the Order of the Arrow while they

Volunteer service in Scouting can become a lifelong interest and a fascinating hobby that fulfills one of the highest callings of good citizenship. Arrowmen who are oriented in service to their fellowmen can find a no more worthwhile opportunity than that of giving leadership to boys through Scouting. A great many of the Scoutmasters, Cubmasters, Explorer Advisors, and their assistants of tomorrow are now active members of the Order of the Arrow. "He alone is worthy to wear the arrow, who will continue faithfully to serve his fellowmen."

continue their education. Arrowmen may take advantage of keeping their membership by joining the College Scouter Reserve through their local council office.

Professional Scouting service

Volunteer leadership in Scouting

A number of Order of the Arrow members find that volunteer leadership positions in Scouting present a challenging opportunity. Councils are interested in recruiting men to serve as unit leaders, unit committeemen, commissioners, merit badge counselors, and for many other positions on district and council committees. Scouters, serving in any capacity, can continue their active membership in an Order of the Arrow lodge.

Arrowmen who find enjoyment in service, working with other people, and who are interested in a worthwhile career should consider the possibilities in the professional service of the Boy Scouts of America. Your Scout executive or a member of the council staff will be glad to talk to you about making preparations to apply for a position as a district Scout executive.

Young men who are seriously interested can help themselves by continuing to give active leadership in their own unit, their Order

matter of choosing courses that will be helpful in planning a career in Scouting. There are some scholarships available, and several colleges offer special courses in youth leadership. All members of the professional family of Scouting are willing to talk to those interested about their educational preparations.

In general, the requirements for a man entering the professional service are that he be a graduate of an accredited college or university and have experience in Scouting as an active member, either as a Scout, Explorer, or a volunteer leader. He must be over 21 years of age and under 35 and have a background of good citizenship, sincere religious convictions, and recommendations from several people who know him well. If approved for the professional service, the applicant must complete the National Executive Institute course for Professional Leaders at Schiff Scout Reservation in Mendham, N. J. He is then eligible for a commission to become a professional leader in Scouting. A large number of men who are now members of the professional service were inducted into the Order of the Arrow during their younger days in a Scout troop or Explorer post as Boy Scouts or Explorers.

of the Arrow lodge, and all Scouting affairs of their home district and local council. Serving as a camp staff member is one of the best ways to become better prepared for a Scouting career. Advancement in Scout rank is helpful in becoming better acquainted with the program.

High school and college counselors will be glad to discuss the

CHEERFUL SERVICE

A Scout Is Cheerful. He smiles whenever he can. His obedience to orders is prompt and cheery. He never shirks or grumbles at hardships.

A Scout Is Helpful. He must be prepared at any time to save life, help injured persons, and share the home duties. He must do at least one Good Turn to somebody every day.

RANACHQUA

COLONNEH LODGE
137
WWW

CHAPTER TEN

INSIGNIA, LITERATURE, AND INDIAN COSTUMES

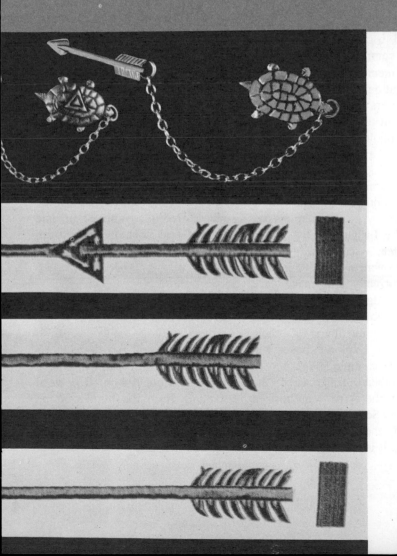

Arrow members are elected by their own units as Scouts or Explorers who best live up to the principles of the Scout Oath and Law in their daily lives. They are chosen not only for what they have done, but also for what they are expected to do. It is, therefore, the responsibility of each Arrowman to continue to set a good example for his fellow unit members and to give leadership in the field of camping.

Each member of the Order has an obligation to his fellow Scouts or Explorers in his own unit and throughout the district and council to uphold the ideals of the Scout Oath and Law. One service he can render to Scouting is to wear his uniform correctly and encourage other boys and leaders to adhere to the regulations set up by the Insignia and Uniform Committee.

If Arrowmen wear their uniforms correctly and make sure that all badges, awards, and insignia are worn in the right places, then other members of their troops and Explorer posts will follow this example.

The official insignia of the Order of the Arrow, authorized by the Boy Scouts of America, are some of the most colorful in Scouting. It is the responsibility of all Arrow members to wear them proudly and correctly.

Ordering materials

The Supply Division, Boy Scouts of America, carries official Arrow insignia, literature, and supplies. All orders must clear through, and be placed by, the local council office. No orders can be accepted from individuals or from lodges. Official Order of the Arrow order forms must always be used.

The official jeweler J. E. Caldwell and Company, Chestnut and Juniper Streets, Philadelphia, Pa., carries the following items: Brotherhood pins, Vigil Honor pins of lodge totem type, and special Arrow jewelry. Orders must be placed well in advance of the date needed and should be approved by the Scout executive.

Universal Arrow badge

The universal Arrow badge is a silver arrow suspended from a red and white ribbon. It is worn hanging from the button of the right breast pocket of the uniform shirt or coat. This badge is worn by all members of the Order—

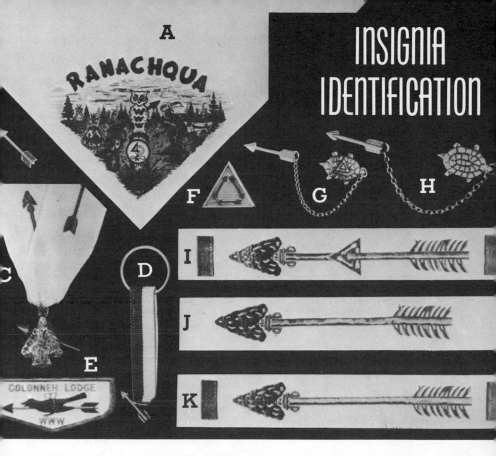

INSIGNIA IDENTIFICATION

A. Lodge neckerchief

B. Order of the Arrow pin for civilian wear

C. Distinguished Service Award

D. Universal Arrow badge for uniform wear

E. Lodge pocket flap patch

F. Vigil Honor pin for civilian wear

G. Vigil Honor totem pin for civilian wear

H. Brotherhood pin for civilian wear

I. Vigil Honor sash

J. Ordeal sash

K. Brotherhood sash

Ordeal, Brotherhood, or Vigil members.

The Arrow pins

The Arrow pins are for non-uniform wear. This simple sterling silver arrow lapel pin may be worn by all members of the Order of the Arrow. Brotherhood members may wear a special totem pin with an Arrow guard attached. Vigil Honor members may wear a totem pin with Vigil Honor triangular insignia superimposed with arrow guard attached. Vigil members may also wear a Vigil Honor pin or lapel button with gold-filled arrows. If desired, a triangle may be superimposed on the totem of the Brotherhood pin and this may then be used as a Vigil Honor pin.

Arrow sashes

The Ordeal Arrow sash is a white band embroidered with a red arrow.

The Brotherhood Arrow sash is similar to the Ordeal sash except that the red arrow is enclosed by two horizontal stripes—one above and one below the arrow. This sash will be worn by Brotherhood members only.

The Vigil Honor sash has a red triangle in the center with three white arrows. It is worn by Vigil Honor members only.

All sashes are worn with the arrow pointing over the right shoulder. They may not be altered in any way, and no other badges are to be worn on them, with the exception of the 50th Anniversary Award.

The Arrow sash is worn only at Order of the Arrow functions. It is not to be worn at troop meetings or other Scout functions unless specifically requested by the lodge chief in cases where members should be identified as rendering special service.

Arrow jewelry

Special rings, charms, and other personal items bearing the lodge totem are available and are frequently purchased for presentation to retiring lodge chiefs or other officers. Order through J. E. Caldwell and Company.

Distinguished Service Award

The Distinguished Service Award is a cast silver arrowhead with an arrow aimed through it. The arrowhead is suspended on a white ribbon embroidered with red arrows and is worn around the neck. It is used for both uniform and nonuniform wear.

A special certificate accompanies the award.

Order of the Arrow neckerchiefs

The local lodge may wish to design a neckerchief for its members. Most lodge neckerchiefs display the lodge totem and lodge name, but other items such as the council or red arrow decorations may be included. Such neckerchiefs are for use only at Order of the Arrow functions or when the lodge is performing a specific service project approved by the lodge chief.

Special neckerchiefs may be secured through the Supply Division. These can be made up in any specific design requested.

Lodge pocket flap patch

Cloth lodge emblems are made available by most local lodges. They are usually embroidered, showing the name and totem of the lodge. It is required by the Insignia and Uniform Committee that these emblems be made to fit the shape of the right shirt pocket flap. The fact that the committee reserves this part of the uniform for an Arrow patch is a compliment to the Order of the Arrow. The Supply Division can provide these patches in any design and color combination.

Indian ceremonial costumes

One of the most fascinating features of the Order of the Arrow is its wide use of Indian costumes by ceremonial teams. A number of lodges have also developed dance teams that lend color and atmosphere to ceremonies and give the lodge a show piece. The dance teams are used as a morale feature in the same way that colorful marching bands are used at high-school and college football games. Indian lore, costuming, and Indian terminology are not the main-line theme of the Order, but it is a part of the program, and many boys are interested in the history, traditions, and customs of the American Indians. The study of Indian lore has become a popular hobby for a number of boys and men who first became interested in this subject through their Order of the Arrow membership.

Local lodges are encouraged to study the customs of the Indian tribes that previously lived in the area of their council territory and, if possible, to model their costumes after those worn by local tribes. Committees have been appointed in some lodges to conduct a research study by checking with local libraries, museums, and enlisting the help of experts on Indian lore. A number of colleges and universities have literature, exhibits, and archives that interested persons may study for information on authentic Indian costumes.

While it is preferable for a lodge to follow the general costuming practices of the Indian tribes of their home area, it is acceptable to adopt a typical pattern for costumes such as those worn by the Plains Indians. Ceremonial team costumes should all represent the same general tribal group.

There should be a definite distinction between the costumes worn by the Allowat Sakima, Mighty Chief, and Meteu, the Medicine Man. Nutiket, the Guard, and Kichkinet, the Guide, would naturally be dressed in less elaborate costumes than the principals. Where Plains Indian costumes are worn, it is suggested that Allowat Sakima wear a double-tailed war bonnet, war shirt, and leggings. A horned single-tail bonnet, war shirt, and leggings should be worn by Meteu. Nutiket and Kichkinet should wear war bonnets without tails, a breechcloth or dance apron, and leggings. All other members of the ceremonial team should wear a roach or coup feather, breechcloth or dance apron. Each of the groups may wear such accessories as necklaces, belts, leg bands, arm bands, and moccasins.

Members of the lodge who have previously served on ceremonial teams and lodge or chapter officers may wear their costumes during ceremonial gatherings. It is further suggested that all other members not actually taking part in the ceremony be dressed in full Scout or Explorer uniforms and wear their Order of the Arrow bands.

Costume making

Leather is an ideal material for making the clothing of the costume, but in recent years it has been rather expensive and difficult to obtain. If you are able to obtain leather, preference is given to the softer types such as the suedes and split calf. Many costume makers put the rough unfinished

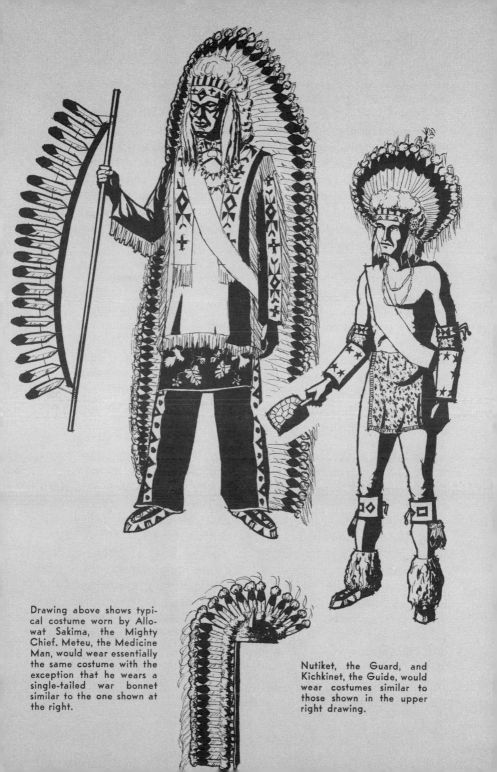

Drawing above shows typical costume worn by Allowat Sakima, the Mighty Chief. Meteu, the Medicine Man, would wear essentially the same costume with the exception that he wears a single-tailed war bonnet similar to the one shown at the right.

Nutiket, the Guard, and Kichkinet, the Guide, would wear costumes similar to those shown in the upper right drawing.

inside to the exterior to give the natural rustic appearance. Shades may vary from light tans to dark cocoa browns.

Ornamentation may be made with beads, appliqué work, dyed cloths, imitation beadwork, metalwork or shellwork. Bear claws or claws of various birds, particularly the eagle and hawk or their imitations made of wood or certain seeds, can also be used. It is here that each lodge may use its own ingenuity in line with the motif used by the tribe of their adoption. The prime requisite in making a good costume is not the money to buy the material but contriving to make less costly material look like the real thing.

Sources of materials

The Supply Division of the Boy Scouts of America is our source of the various materials necessary to make costumes.

In addition, you can contact local leather-goods manufacturers, particularly those making leather jackets; feather merchants, who normally supply materials for ornamentation of women's hats; bead importers; and stockyards for horns. Incidentally, your own butcher can supply you with turkey and goose feathers and possibly rooster spurs, which when enameled black or dark brown make fine imitations of bear claws. Chicken bones, when properly cut into equal lengths and bleached, make fine, natural-looking long beads for necklaces. Long straight chicken or turkey bones and even the stems from corncob pipes make an excellent material for Indian breastplates.

Improvised materials

Costume and properties for your lodge ceremonies can be as expensive or inexpensive as you wish to make them. If you wish to start off modestly and experiment with cheaper materials before going into costume making with genuine leather and other expensive items of ornamentation, you can use many materials found right in your own home.

Any ordinary cloth, old shirts or suits, scrap pieces of broadcloth, old draperies, curtains and various upholstery fabrics can be used for vests, leggings, or chaps by the simple process of a little cutting, sewing, dyeing, and fringing. Pinking shears are most useful for cutting a toothed edge so that cloth will not unravel.

Remember that the Indians did not always have prime materials

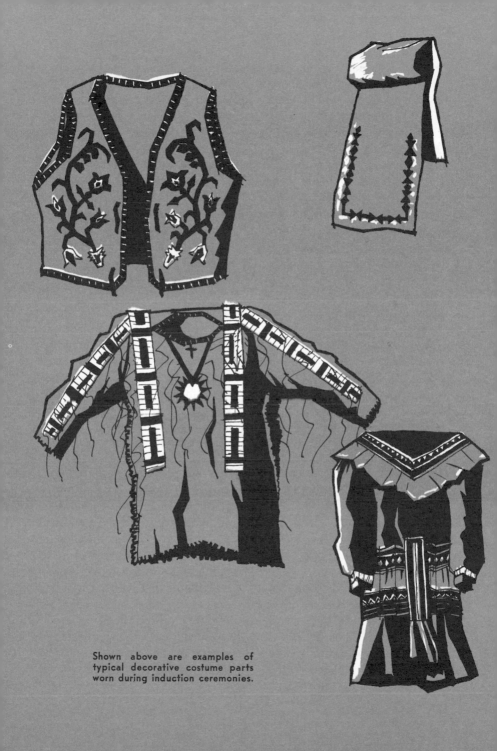

Shown above are examples of typical decorative costume parts worn during induction ceremonies.

on hand, and many of them took old cloth shirts and dyed them a bright color and wore them as proudly as the chief with the elk-skin war shirt. Appliqué colored cloth onto your costume, particularly onto the leggings and breech-cloth, and you will get a fine effect. Pieces of old metal can be worked into arm bands and other decorations. Bells can be made from empty shotgun shells, casings, or thin metal rolled into a cone shape.

Pieces of fur, even ermine scraps or unused tails, can be obtained from your local furrier. Maybe your mother has an old beaded bag or dress that can be used to get desired effects. Check on the stockyard for cow or calf teeth.

Remember that the Indian improvised and even copied from the white man when he saw something that he liked. You will find that imagination is your biggest asset.

Makeup

The Indian used paint as a symbolic interpretation of the mysteries of nature, and in a desire to beautify himself.

As a rule the primary colors were used, and he secured them from natural sources. Each color had its general classification and meaning. Thus, as a rule, black meant death in some form, red signified war, white stood for peace.

In the ceremonies of the Order of the Arrow our use of makeup is essentially to create an atmosphere for the legendary background of our Order. Makeup should be used as an aid to the costuming to create an appropriate setting for the ceremonial.

Different Indian tribes varied in methods of painting themselves, but generally the methods were much the same. Therefore, in our makeup it would be well to study the customs and methods used in our particular locality, keeping in mind that we, too, have a medicine man, a mighty chief, a guide, and a guardian.

If you wish to brown the face and body, it is suggested that you use professional makeup. This can be provided in stick, powder, or liquid form from a theatrical supply house or a supplier of Indian-craft materials. Be sure to purchase a water-soluble paint to make removing it easier. Among the best-known manufacturers are Max Factor and Stein.

For design work you will need several of the basic colors. If you use the stick type of grease paint, it is a good idea to mix some of it with cold cream. Form a smooth paste by mixing it with a spatula. In this way you can also mix all the colors that you want and store them in jars for future use, so that they will not dry out. This method has the advantage of making the grease paint easy to apply and remarkably easy to remove. Matchsticks with a little cotton twisted on the end or, even better yet, pipe cleaners folded in half, using the looped end, make excellent applicators. Warning! If you use the color stick directly, not mixing in the cold cream, grease the skin first with cold cream, remove the excess cream, and then you will not have difficulty in getting the paint off. The Supply Division makes available color sticks that are water soluble and require no cold cream. Just use soap and water.

In your choice of colors and design you must consider the lighting effects. Since your light source will probably consist of a fire and candles, sharp color contrasts are necessary. Too gaudy or startling an effect detracts from the purpose for which you are striving—a serious and beautiful ceremony. It is sensible, therefore, to use one, two, or three colors.

The Indian used symbolic and geometrical designs as the basis of his makeup. Each design and color had its meaning and was his interpretation of the meaning he wished to express to others. You can get ideas for your makeup from pictures of actual Indians and from various books on Indian lore.

Accessories

The accessories to the costuming and to the property setup are just as important as the main features. They dress up and embellish the entire show.

We must have torches to supplement the stationary council fires. There are two important types and each has its own use. For permanent reading and for general illumination a long-pole torch is required. This is easily constructed by stuffing a tin can with cotton waste or old rags and saturating it with kerosine. The can is suspended by a piece of baling wire, attached as the handle on a pail, with the wire attached to a pole at least 6 feet high, so that the can swings freely between the upturned arms of the wire support. This free-swinging device allows the torch to be dipped down for reading purposes while the can stays in an upright position, so that the stuffing will

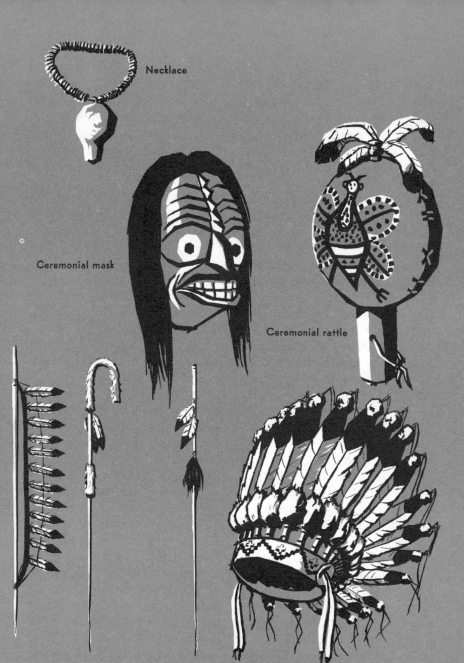

Necklace

Ceremonial mask

Ceremonial rattle

Coupsticks

War bonnet

not fall out. (Read only lists of candidates, special announcements, etc. Ceremonies should be thoroughly memorized.)

The other type of torch is more rustic and natural and is preferred where the materials are available. It can be made by simply hollowing out a pine knot on the thick end so that cotton waste or old rags can be stuffed in tightly. Check to see that there is no hole all the way through the center and that there are no cracks in the walls that will permit kerosine to seep through. The seeping kerosine may be ignited and cause a severe burn. The pine knots can be found in old fallen trees that have decayed. The knots, being tougher than the rest of the tree, are usually in a good state of preservation and can be easily knocked loose from the rest of the tree. These torches make a beautiful sight, especially when held aloft by members leading candidates or other groups through the woods, and are used for illumination and reading at the ceremonial grounds.

No Indian ceremony is complete without the cadence of the tom-tom. When properly handled it adds much to the impressiveness of the ceremony. The tom-toms can be ornamented and painted with various symbolic signs.

Coupsticks, war clubs, rattles, anklet bells, and even a peace pipe can be used to round out the dignity and authenticity of the ceremony. A tepee in the background also adds greatly to the general atmosphere.

Let us catch the higher vision.
Let us find the greater beauty
In the life of cheerful service.

Ordeal

HELPFUL LITERATURE

Items with catalog numbers are available from the Supply Division. Those without catalog numbers may be obtained from local bookstores or libraries.

Order of the Arrow literature

Order of the Arrow Handbook, No. 5000
Ordeal Ceremony, No. 5005
Brotherhood Ceremony, No. 5006
Questionnaire for Examination of Candidates for Brotherhood Membership, No. 5007
Ceremony for the Vigil Honor, No. 5043
Order of the Arrow (membership card), No. 5008
Order of the Arrow—Information for New Members, No. 5004
Order of the Arrow (information leaflet), No. 5031
Order of the Arrow Record Book, No. 5038

Indian lore books

American Indian Crafts— Ralph Hubbard
This pamphlet by a famous Indian writer is worth owning and contains explanations and sketches of costuming and all accessories. It has a fine bibliography. Can be obtained from Plume Trading and Sales Company, P.O. Box 585, Monroe, N. Y. 10950.

Book of Indian-Crafts and Customs, The—Bernard S. Mason No. 3588
One of the best books on costuming techniques. Profusely illustrated.

Book of Indian Crafts and Indian Lore, The—Julian Harris Salomon, No. 3514
This is a very comprehensive

112

book and is probably the most outstanding work of its type. It is highly recommended. It covers all the tribes of the country and has many fine sketches and pictures.

Book of Woodcraft — Ernest Thompson Seton
A fine, general outdoor book with interesting parts on Indian lore. Some good council-fire setups, as well as costume techniques.

Buckskin Book for Buckskin Men and Boys — Dan Beard
Uncle Dan at his best. He knew boy-talk. There are plenty of sketches and plenty of know-how talk about items not covered in other books.

Costumes Throughout the Ages — Mary Evans
Pages 304-8 for different types of Indian dress throughout the country.

Dances and Stories of the American Indian—Bernard S. Mason, No. 3581
Dances and showmanship.

Dancing Gods: Indian Ceremonies of New Mexico and Arizona — Erna Fergusson
Culture and ceremonies of the Southwest Indians.

Indian and Camp Handicraft— W. Ben Hunt, No. 3531
In this opus are found plates on bonnets and beadwork, as well as general handicraft.

Indian How Book, The — Arthur C. Parker
General Indian know-how source book.

Indian Lore, BL-84
A collection of articles by W. Ben Hunt reprinted from *Boys' Life* magazine. Available from *Boys' Life,* New Brunswick, N. J. 08903.

Indian Lore, merit badge pamphlet, No. 3358A
One of the best survey books on Indian culture and customs. Tells of the various tribes and their location in North America.

North American Indians of the Plains—Clark Wissler
A good general reference by a one-time student of Indian lore.

Rhythm of the Redman, The— Julia M. Buttree, No. 3587
Songs and dances only.

Wildwood Wisdom—Ellsworth Jaeger

ENGLISH — LENNI LENAPE PRONUNCIATION GUIDE

YOUR INDIAN NAME

What is an Indian name?'
Is it just a childish game?
  No, indeed! It means much more;
  It's all you've ever been before;
  It's all the future has in store.
It's really what you truly are—
Your secret self, your guiding star.
  It's what all others think of you;
  It's what you say and what you do,
  What you think, what dreams you see,
  And all you ever hope to be.
  It's rocks and lakes and mountains grand,
  And sounds that wild things understand;
  The mighty eagle, high above,
  The dauntless hawk, the cooing dove,
  The cunning fox, the wise, strong bear,
  The scent of pine-smoke in the air,
  The running deer, the bounding hare,
  The autumn forest, bright and still,
  The wind that blows where e'er it will,
  A ring of tipis by a hill.
  The sudden war cry, rising higher,
  The pipe that never crosses fire;
  The winter meat rack, bare and grim,
  The chant that echoes like a hymn.
  The pulsing beat of tom-tom's voice,
  The Crow-Moon Sun that cries "Rejoice!"
  The colored sand on hogan floor,
  The hatchet, red with foeman's gore;
  The banded maize, the turquoise ring,
  The Vict'ry Song, the all-night sing;
  Down through every clime and age,
  Part of our Nation's heritage,
  The chieftain, warrior, squaw and sage,
  The knife that cuts the treaty page;
  From Vera Cruz to Wounded Knee
  All the Indian wished to be,
  All he felt, could hear, could see,
  Indelible, with wise, wild hand,
  He has left upon our land.
  And this is what, good friend, you claim
  When you receive your Indian name.

                              by *Sue Drexel*

114

Vigil Honor committees have a responsibility to choose Indian names for their new Vigil Honor candidates. It is recommended that the Vigil names be chosen from the language of Indian tribes whose traditional homes were in the area of the local council where the lodge operates. A partial list of names in the language of the Lenni Lenape is printed here for local use in case Indian-English translations are not available to lodges in some areas.

The Lenape translations were taken from *A Lenape-English Dictionary,* by Daniel G. Brinton, A.M., M.D., and the Reverend Albert S. Anthony, published by the Historical Society of Pennsylvania, in 1888.

It is interesting to note that the original translation of the Lenape language into English was made by missionaries of the Moravian Church. These pioneers in bringing Western civilization and Christianity to the native Indians of the Delaware Valley were Dutch and German. This may account for the gutteral sounds and some of the difficulty encountered by English-speaking people in pronunciation of the Lenape tongue.

The Delaware River, Delaware Bay, and the state of Delaware were named for Sir Thomas West, the third Lord *De la Warre,* an early governor of Virginia. Later the Indians who lived in the river valley became known as the Delawares. Actually, these people were the Lenni Lenape.

Regarding pronunciation of the Lenape tongue, the *Lenape-English Dictionary* has this to say:

"As is well known, the early Moravians were exclusively Germans; and in reducing the Lenape to a written idiom they made use of the German alphabet, without adding to it any phonetic signs. This alphabet was not ill adapted for the purpose. It could represent the gutterals and the vowel sounds of the Lenape with sufficient clearness.

ENGLISH — LENNI LENAPE WORD LIST

A

Able, One Who Is Able	Wunita
Accomplished One	Pakantschiechen
Active One	Wischixin
Adviser	Witatschimolsin
Afoot, He Who Goes Afoot	Pommissin
Aged One	Kikey
Agreeable One	Nachgundin
Agrees, He Who Agrees	Nguttitehen
Aids, One Who Aids	Witäwematpanni
Alder Tree	Topi
Alone, One Who Is Alone	Nechoha
Ardent One	Segachtek
Arrow	Alluns
Assists, One Who Assists	Witschindin
Assistant	Witawematpanni
Assures, One Who	Kittaptonen
Attention, One Who Gets Attention	Papenauwelendam
Authority, One Who Has Authority	Tschitanessoagan
Away, He Who Goes Away	Elemussit

B

Bachelor	Kikape
Back, One Who Comes Back	Apatschin
Badger	Gawi
Bald-Headed One	Moschakantpeu
Bald Eagle	Woapalanne
Bear	Machque
Bearded One	Tuney
Beaver	Ktemaque
Bee	Amoe

Behaves, He Who Behaves Well	Wulilissin
Believer	Olsittam
Beloved	Ahotasu
Best	Wulit
Beyond, He Who Looks Beyond	Wulowachtauwoapin
Big	Amangi
Birch Tree	Wihhinachk
Bird	Awehhelleu
Bird, Blackbird	Tskennak
Bird, Redbird	Mehokquiman
Black	Sukeu
Black Fish	Sukamek
Black Fox	Wulalowe
Black Snake	Sukachgook
Blameless One	Kschiechelensin
Blamelessly, He Who Lives Blamelessly	Wawulauchsin
Blessed One	Welapensit
Blue	Schiwapew
Bluebird	Tschimalus
Boat	Amochol
Book	Bambil
Book Reader	Achgindamen
Boulder	Ganschapuchk
Bow (as in bow and arrow)	Hattape
Boy	Skahenso
Boy, Big Boy	Pilapeu
Boy, Little Boy	Pilawetit
Bright	Wachejeu
Broad	Achgameu
Brother	Nimat
Brother, Elder Brother	Chans
Brother, Younger Brother	Chesimus
Brotherhood	Wimachtendienk
Brown	Wipungweu
Buck (deer)	Ajapeu
Buffalo	Sisilija
Builder	Wikhetschik
Bullfrog	Oleleu
Business Manager	Nanatschitaquik
Busy One	Wischiki
Buys, One Who Buys	Ajummen
Buzzard, Turkey Buzzard	Amatschipuis

C

Calm Minded One	Klamhattenamin
Camper	Mechmauwikenk
Canoe, Little Canoe	Amocholes
Capable One	Tschitanissowagan

116

Captain	Lachxowilenno
Carefree One	Ksinelendam
Careful One	Nechasin
Cares, One Who Cares	Anatschiton
Cat, Wildcat	Nianque
Cattle Owner	Wdallemunsit
Cautious One	Anatschihuwewagan
Cedar, Red Cedar Tree	Mehokhokus
Cedar, White Cedar Tree	Talala
Certain, One Who Is Certain	Awelendam
Chestnut Tree	Woapiminschi
Chief	Sakima
Chief, Head Chief	Gegeyjumhet
Chief, Mighty Chief	Allowat Sakima
Child	Amemens
Chipmunk	Anicus
Chosen, One	Gegekhuntschik
Clean One	Kschiechek
Cloud	Achgumhok
Clown	Gebtschaat
Cold One	Taquatschin
Collector	Mawachpo
Comes Back, He Who Comes Back	Apatschin
Comforts, One Who Comforts	Wulilaweman
Companion	Nitis
Comrade	Tschutti
Concerned, He Who Is Concerned	
	Lachauweleman
Confidence, One Who Has Confidence	
	Nageuchsowagan
Contented One	Tepelendam
Cook	Sachgachtoon
Cordial One	Wdehiwi
Counsels, One Who Holds Councils	
	Witatschimolsin
Counselor	Atschimolsin
Crane	Taleka
Creates, One Who Creates with Hands	
	Gischihan
Creates, One Who Creates with Mind	
	Gischeleman
Cries, One Who Cries Aloud	Ganschiechsin
Crow	Ahas
Cures, One Who Cures	Kikehuwet
Current, Strong Current	Kschippehellen
Cutter of Wood	Manachewagan

D

Dancer	Gentgeen
Deer	Achtu

Deer, Young Deer	Mamalis
Delights, One Who Delights	Winginamen
Delivers, One Who Delivers	Nihillasohen
Determined One	Gischitehen
Different One	Tschetschpi
Diligent One	Lilchpin
Discerning One	Natenummen
Doctor	Kikehuwet
Dog	Allum
Dog, Little Dog	Allumes
Doorkeeper	Nutschisquandawet
Doubtful One	Quilawelensin
Dove	Amimi
Dove, Wild Dove	Mowichleu
Dreamer	Lungwamen
Drum Beater	Pohonasin

E

Eagle, Bald Eagle	Woapalanne
Earnest One	Kittelendamwagan
East Wind	Achpateuny
Easily, One Who Thinks Easily	Apuelendam
Easy One	Ksinelendam
Eater	Mizin
Eight	Chaasch
Elder	Kikeyjumhet
Elder Brother	Chans
Elected One	Gegekhuntschik
Elk	Mos
Elm Tree	Achgikbi
Encourages, One Who Encourages	Gihim
Endurance, He Who Has Endurance	
	Ahowoapewi
Endures, He Who Endures Pain	
	Mamchachwelendam
Enjoys, One Who Enjoys	Apendamen
Enjoyable One	Apensuwi
Enlightens, One Who Enlightens	
	Gischachsummen
Established, One Who Is Established	
	Tschitanigachen
Esteemed One	Ahoatam
Esteemed, One Who Is Highly Esteemed	
	Allowelendam
Excellent One	Wdallowelemuwi
Excited One	Glakelendam
Exerts, One Who Exerts Himself	Wischixin
Exhorts, One Who Exhorts	Guntschitagen
Experienced One	Lippoe
Extravagant One	Klakelendam

F

Farmer	Hakihet
Farsighted One	Wulowachtauwoapin
Fast One	Tschitanek
Father, One Who Is a Father	Wetochwink
Fifth	Palenachtchegit
Fighter	Machtagen
Fine One	Awullsu
Fire Maker	Tindeuchen
Fireman	Atenkpatton
Firm One	Tschitanigachen
First	Netami
First Aid, He Who Gives First Aid	
	Achibis
Fish	Names
Fish, Large Fish	Amangamek
Fisherman	Wendamen
Five	Palenach
Flies, One Who Flies	Wschimuin
Follower	Nosogamen
Foremost One	Niganit
Forgetful One	Wannessin
Forceful One	Achtschinkhalan
Four	Newo
Fourth	Neweleneyit
Fox, Black Fox	Wulalowe
Fox, Gray Fox	Woakus
Friend	Elangomat
Friendly One	Tgauchsin
Friendly Looking One	Langomuwinaxin
Frog	Tsquall

G

Gardner	Menhakehhamat
Generous One	Wilawilihan
Gentle One	Wulamehelleu

Good, He Who Does Good for Others	
	Wulihan
Good One	Awullsu
Good Natured One	Tgauchsin
Goose, Wild Goose	Kaak
Gracious One	Eluwilissit
Grateful One	Genamuwi
Gray	Wipunxit
Gray-Headed One	Wapantpeu lenno
Gray Hair	Woaphokquawon
Good-Looking One	Wulinaxin
Great One	Amangi
Green	Asgask
Grows, One Who Grows Fast	Lachpikin
Groundhog	Gawi
Guard	Nutiket
Guide	Kichkinet

H

Hair, Gray Hair	Woaphokquawon
Handsome One	Wulisso
Happy, He Who Makes Others Happy	
	Lauchsoheen
Happy One	Wulamallessin
Hawk	Meechgalanne
Hawk, Fish Hawk	Nimenees
Helper	Witschindin
Hears, One Who Hears Well	Achginchen
Heart	Wdee
Helpful One	Witscheman
Hiker	Achpamsin
Honest One	Schachachgapewi
Honorable One	Wulapeju
Honored One	Machelemuxit
Hopeful One	Nageuchsin
Horse	Nenajunges
Horseback Rider	Nenajungeshammen
How, One Who Knows How	Wunita
Humble One	Gettemagelensit
Humility, One Who Has Humility	
	Tangitehewagan
Hungry One	Gattopuin
Hunter	Elauwit

I

Indifferent One	Ajanhelendam
Inquiring One	Natoochton
Instructs, One Who Instructs	Allohakasin
Interpreter	Anhoktonhen

J

Just One	Wulapeju
Joyful One	Wulelendam
Jocular One	Achgiguwen

K

Kind One	Wulilisseu
King, Great King	Kittakima
Kinsman	Langoma
Knowledge, One Who Has Knowledge	
	Weuchsowagan
Knows, One Who Knows How	Wunita

L

Lamp	Nendawagan
Lamp Carrier	Nendawen
Large One	Amangi
Laughing One	Gilkissin
Leader	Takachsin
Lifesaver	Gachpallan
Lifts, One Who Lifts Up	Aspenummen
Listener	Glistam
Little One	Tatchen
Lively One	Achgiguwen
Load, One Who Carries a Load	Najundam
Long One	Amiga
Looks, One Who Looks Fine	Wulinaxin
Loving One	Ahoaltuwi
Loyal One	Leke
Lucky One	Welapensit

M

Makes, He Who Makes	Gischihan
Man	Lenno
Man, Little Man	Lennotit
Man, Old Man	Mihillusis
Mediator	Etschihillat
Medicine Man	Meteu
Merchant	Memhallamund
Merciful One	Achgettemagelo
Merry One	Wulelendam
Messenger	Elogamgussit
Mighty One	Allouchsit
Mighty and Powerful One	Ehalluchsit
Mild One	Tgauchsu
Mind, One of Calm Mind	Klamhattenamin
Minded, High-Minded One	Machelensin

Minister	Pichpemmetonhet
Modest One	Tachpachiwi
Mountain	Wachtschu
Mouse	Achpoques
Muskrat	Damaskus

N

Neighbor	Pechotschigalit
Nephew	Longachsiss
Night Hawk	Pischk
Nimble One	Wischixin
Nine	Peschgonk
Noisy One	Achgiguwen
North	Lowaneu
Nurse	Nechnutschinget

O

Oak, Black Oak	Wisachgak
Oak, White Oak	Wipunquoak
Obedient One	Awullsittamuwi
One	Mawat
Opossum	Woapink
Otter	Gunammochk
Overseer	Genachgihat
Owl	Gokhos
Owl, Little Owl	Gokhotit

P

Pale One	Woaptigihilleu
Panther	Quenischquney
Parent	Wenitschanit
Partridge	Popokus
Patient One	Papesu
Pays, One Who Pays	Eenhen
Peaceable One	Achwangundowi
Peaceful One	Langundowi
Perplexed One	Ksukquamallsin
Persevering One	Tschitanitehen
Physician	Kikehuwet
Pigeon	Amemi
Pine Tree	Kuwe
Pious One	Welilissit
Plenty, One Who Has Plenty	Wiaxowagan
Poplar Tree	Amocholhe
Power, He Who Has Spiritual Power	
	Mantowagan
Powerful One	Allohak

Righteous One	Schachachgapewi
Robin	Tschisgokus
Rock	Achsin
Rock, Big Rock	Ganschapuchk
Runner, Fast Runner	Kschamehhellan

S

Sacrifices, One Who Sacrifices	Wihungen
Sad One	Sakquelendam
Satisfied One	Gispuin
Searches, One Who Searches	Lattoniken
Second	Nischeneyit
Secretary	Lekhiket
Seeker	Elachtoniket
Sees, He Who Sees	Nemen
Sensitive One	Amandamuwi
Servant of the Lord	Allogagan Nehellatank
Serves, He Who Serves	Allogagan
Seven	Nischasch
Shepherd	Nutemekiset
Silent One	Tschitgussin
Sings, One Who Sings	Nachgohuman
Six	Guttasch
Skillful One	Wowoatam
Small One	Tangetto
Snake	Achgook
Son	Quis
Sorrowful One	Uschuwelendam
Speaker, Fast Speaker	Lachpiechsin
Speaker, Loud Speaker	Amangiechsin
Speaks, He Who Speaks Favorably	
	Wulaptonen
Speaks, He Who Speaks Truly	Wulamoe
Spirits, He Who Has Good Spirits	
	Wulantowagan
Spiritual One	Achewon
Spiritual, One Who Has Spiritual Power	
	Mantowagan
Spruce Tree	Schind
Square One	Haschawije
Squirrel, Flying Squirrel	Blaknik
Squirrel, Ground Squirrel	Anicus
Squirrel, Red Squirrel	Kuwewanik
Star	Allanque
Steady One	Clamhattenmoagan
Stone	Achsin
Stranger	Tschepsit
Stronger	Tschitani
Strengthens, One Who Strengthens	
	Tschitanissohen

Powerful, Most Powerful One	Eluwak
Praised, One Who Is Praised	
	Wulakenimgussin
Praises, He Who Praises	Amentschinsin
Pretty One	Awullsu
Preacher	Pichpemmetonhet
Prepared, He Who Is Prepared	Gischenaxin
Promise, He Who Keeps a Promise	Wulamoen
Proud One	Wulelensin
Persuades, One Who Persuades	
	Achtschinkhalan
Prudent One	Wewoatamowi
Puppy	Allumes

Q

Quick One	Allapijeyjuwagan
Quiet One	Klamachpin

R

Rabbit	Moskimus
Raccoon	Espan
Rattlesnake	Wischalowe
Reader	Achkindiken
Ready, One Who Is Ready	Gischhatteu
Recommended, One Who Is Recommended	
	Wulakenimgussin
Red	Machkeu
Redbird	Mehokquiman
Redheaded One	Meechgalhukquot
Reliable One	Nagatamen
Remembers, He Who Remembers	
	Meschatamen
Rests, He Who Rests	Alachimuin
Returns, He Who Returns	Apatschin
Rich Man	Pawallessin

Strong One	Achewon	Violin Player	Achpiquon
Sure One	Bischik	Visitor	Kiwikaman
Swiftly, He Who Goes Swiftly	Kschihillen		
Swimmer	Aschowin		

W

Waits, He Who Waits	Pesoop
Walker	Pemsit
Walker, Fast Walker	Kschochwen
Walks, He Who Walks Alone	Nechochwen
Warrior	Netopalis
Wasp	Amoe
Watchman	Wewoapisak
Water, Clear Water	Kschiechpecat
Water, Deep Water	Chuppecat
Water, Still Water	Klampeechen
Weasel	Sanquen
Well, He Who Is Always Well	
	Wawulamallessin
Well Behaved	Welauchsit
West	Wundchenneu
Whippoorwill	Quekolis
White	Wapsu
Wide One	Achgameu
Willing One	Nuwingi
Wind, East Wind	Achpateuny
Wind, West Wind	Linchen
Winner	Wsihuwen
Wiseman	Wowoatammowino
Witty One	Luppoewagan
Wonderful One	Wulelemi
Wise One	Lippoe
Wolf	Wiechcheu
Woodcock	Memeu
Woodcutter	Giskhaquen
Wood Gatherer	Natachtu
Woodpecker	Papaches
Woodpecker, Redheaded Woodpecker	
	Memakochkus
Worker	Mikemossit
Work, One Who Does Good Work	
	Wulalogewagan
Worker, Hard Worker	Achowalogen
Worthy One	Elgixin
Wounded One	Achpequot
Writer	Lekhiket

T

Talker	Wewingtonheet
Talker, Fast Talker	Alappiechsin
Tall One	Gunaquot
Teacher	Achgeketum
Ten	Metellen
Thankful One	Genamuwi
Thin One	Waskeu
Thinker	Litchen
Thinker, Deep Thinker	Achowelendam
Thinks, One Who Thinks Easily	Apuelendam
Third	Nechit
Thoughtful One	Pennauweleman
Tired One	Wiquihillau
Toiler	Achowalogen
Torch Carrier	Nendawen
Trader	Memhallmund
Traveler	Memsochet
Traveler, Night Traveler	Nipahwochwen
Travels, He Who Travels Alone	Nechochwen
Treasurer	Mawachpo
Three	Nacha
Troubled, The Troubled One	Sakquelendamen
True, He Who Is True	Leke
True, He Who Has Proven True	Gischileu
Trusted, One Who Can Be Trusted	Nagatamen
Trustworthy One	Nageuchsowagan
Trusts, One Who Trusts	Nhakeuchsin
Truth, Speaker of Truth	Ktschillachton
Truthful One	Wulamoewaganit
Turkey	Tschikenum
Turkey Cock	Bloeu
Turtle	Tulpe
Twin	Gachpees
Two	Nischa

U-V

Upright One	Wulapejuwagan
Useful One	Apensuwi
Unconcerned One	Ajanhelendam
Understanding One	Pendamen
Unlucky One	Pallikteminak
Valor, Man of Valor	Ilau
Valuable One	Wilawi

Y and Z

Yellow	Wisaweu
Younger Brother	Chesimus
Zealous One	Skattek

ORDER OF THE ARROW OFFICIAL SONG
WORDS BY E. URNER GOODMAN

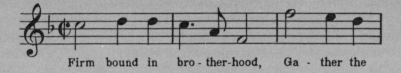

Firm bound in bro - ther-hood, Ga - ther the

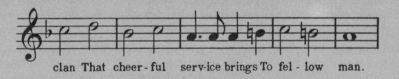

clan That cheer - ful serv-ice brings To fel - low man.

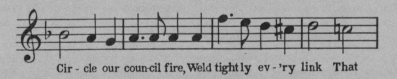

Cir - cle our coun-cil fire, Weld tightly ev - 'ry link That

binds us in bro-ther-hood, Wi - mach - ten - dienk.

INDEX

124

125

NATIONAL ORDER MEETINGS AND OFFICERS

National Meeting	Met at	Date	NATIONAL OFFICERS		
			Chief	Secretary	Treasurer
1	Philadelphia, Pa.	10- 7-21	E. U. Goodman	E. R. Carrick	A. A. Schuck
2	Reading, Pa.	10- 7-22	A. A. Schuck	W. P. Bradley	R. H. Dilks
3	Baltimore, Md.	10-13-23	C. A. Edson	W. A. Stumpp	W. P. Bradley
4	Tuxedo Park, N.Y.	10-31-24	A. C. Nichols, Jr.	H. A. Gordon	J. D. Carstang
5	Treasure Island, N.J.	10-16-25	E. R. Carrick	H. A. Gordon	L. Harrison
6	Reading, Pa.	10-29-26	W. A. Stumpp	H. A. Gordon	H. Birch
7	Kanohwahke Lake, N.Y.	10-14-27	R. S. Henderson	H. A. Gordon	A. Pancoast
8	Philadelphia, Pa.	11-29-29	R. Price	B. J. Thomas	J. N. Pattison III
9	Pilot Knob, N.Y.	9-11-31	R. Price	W. F. Livermore	J. N. Pattison III
10	Owasippe, Mich.	9-10-33	T. G. Cairns	H. L. Nelson	J. N. Pattison III
11	Treasure Island, N.J.	9- 7-36	J. H. Brinton	H. L. Nelson	J. A. Brunton, Jr.
12	Irondale, Mo.	9- 5-38	J. A. Brunton, Jr.	H. L. Nelson	G. A. Mozealous
13	Ligonier, Pa.	9- 2-40	G. A. Mozealous	H. L. Nelson	R. H. Heistand
*	Philadelphia, Pa.	12-27-42	H. L. Nelson	John C. Norsk	R. H. Heistand
14	Chanute Field, Ill.	8-29-46	R. H. Heistand	John C. Norsk	J. R. Newbery
15	Bloomington, Ind.	8-27-48	G. Kellock Hale, appointed national chairman		
16	Bloomington, Ind.	8-30-50	H. Lloyd Nelson, appointed national chairman		
			J. Richard Wilson, national conference chief		
17	Oxford, Ohio	8-29-52	H. Lloyd Nelson, appointed national chairman		
18	Laramie, Wyo.	8-26-54	James R. Montgomery, national conference chief		
			H. Lloyd Nelson, appointed national chairman		
			James R. Feil, national conference chief		
19	Bloomington, Ind.	8-27-56	James P. Hunter, appointed national chairman		
			James L. Waters, national conference chief		
20	Lawrence, Kansas	8-25-58	James P. Hunter, appointed national chairman		
			James W. Kolka, national conference chief		
21	Bloomington, Ind.	8-21-61	L. George Feil, appointed national chairman		
			Ronald J. Temple, national conference chief		
22	Champaign, Ill.	8-20-63	L. George Feil, national chairman		
23	Bloomington, Ind.	8-27-65	Robert B. Ellsperman, national conference chief		
			L. George Feil, national chairman		
			Michael S. Costello, national conference chief		
24	Lincoln, Nebraska	8-28-67	L. George Feil, national chairman		
			Robert F. Szczys, national conference chief		

*In December, 1942, these officers were elected by the National Executive Committee of the Order of the Arrow and reelected in 1944 and 1945, because meetings of the national lodge were not held during the war years

INDIAN CEREMONIAL COSTUME KITS

[A] **INDIAN BEADCRAFT OUTFIT**—Complete kit for weaving colorful beaded items. You get wire loom, beads, needles, thread, and illustrations. **No. 1144 $2.25 No. 1634** Beadloom Set **65¢**

[B] **DANCE BELL KIT**—Braves wore dance bells at tribal dances to stir excitement. Add a pair to your costume for your Indian ceremonies. In kit are ten bells, two 8″ leather straps, long leather thongs, instructions. **No. 2666....$1.50**

[C] **WAR BONNET KIT**—Make and wear big chief's bonnet. Kit contains 30 colorful tail feathers. Choose red, green, black, white, orange, blue or yellow. Kit includes all parts, is fun to assemble.
No. 2603 War Bonnet Kit **$5.25**
No. 2607 War Bonnet Kit (wing feathers) **4.25**

[D] **FEATHER ROACH KIT**—Kit has 28 long feathers, 56 white and 56 red fluffies, other needed materials. Great way to top off your ceremonial costume, make it look real. **No. 2681 ....$4.95**

[E] **FEATHER CREST KIT**—Just like the braves wore! Adds a finishing touch to your Indian costumes. Kit has parts including bright imitation eagle feathers, illustrations. **No. 2682 ....$3.85**

[F] **HAIR ROACH KIT**—Young braves wore this hair roach for tribal dances and rituals. Now you can make one! Kit has mock eagle feather, other parts, and instructions. **No. 2668 ......$1.00**

[G] **APACHE HEADDRESS KIT**—Like to make an Indian-style headdress for your costume? This 4-feather rosette resembles those worn by Apache warriors into battle. Kit has colorful feathers, 30 base fluffies, felt, cement. **No. 2663 ....60¢**

[H] **BEAR CLAW KIT**—Indians valued these highly. Tribal chiefs and medicine men wore them. It's easy to make your own. Plastic claws, colorful beads, leather thong, and instructions.
No. 2616 . . . . **$1.98**

All prices subject to change

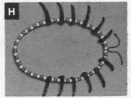

AVAILABLE THROUGH YOUR LOCAL SCOUT DISTRIBUTOR
BOY SCOUTS OF AMERICA · SUPPLY DIVISION

ADD NEW LIFE AND EXCITEMENT TO INDIAN DANCES WITH
Colorful Ceremonial Dress

[A]

[B]

[D]

[A] INDIAN VEST KIT — Attractive vest is perfect for wear by Nutiket, Kichkinet, other members of ceremonial team. Kit has 1¼-yds. of buckskin cloth, one 75″ strip of blue cloth, red felt for cutting designs, patterns. **No. 2610** **$3.00**

[B] INDIAN WAR SHIRT KIT — Plains Indian type of war shirt is tops for wear by Allowat Sakima and Meteu. Kit has 3 yds. of buckskin cloth, one 24″ strip blue felt binding, two each of 36″ and 18″ white felt strips. **No. 2609** **$6.00**

[C] INDIAN LEGGINGS KIT—These leggings of the Plains Indian type are worn by all members of the ceremonial team. Kit contains 2½ yds. of heavy cloth, 4 yds. cloth binding of a contrasting color, and two 36″ felt strips.
No. 2660 Buckskin color cloth **$5.50**
No. 2660A Blue cloth 5.50

INDIAN BREECHCLOTH KIT (not shown) — Matching breechcloth for wear with leggings described above by all members of the ceremonial team. Kit contains one 12″ x 72″ piece of double-napped cloth, one 108″ grosgrain ribbon for binding.
No. 2661 Blue cloth **$1.50**
No. 2661A Red cloth 1.50

[D] INDIAN WAR BONNET KIT — This beautiful headdress is styled after the war bonnets of plains chieftains. It's suitable for wear alone by Nutiket or Kichkinet. (Add Tail Kit, No. 2606, below for greater effectiveness when Allowat Sakima dons it.) Kit has 30 imitation eagle feathers 12″ x 14″ long, white base fluffies, red tip fluffies, other parts, instructions. **No. 2605** **$9.50**

INDIAN WAR BONNET TAIL KIT (not shown) —Single or double tails may be attached to the war bonnet above for wear by the Mighty Chief, Allowat Sakima. Kit holds 30 imitation eagle feathers 12″ to 14″ long, other needed parts. **2606 $9.50**
All prices subject to change

[C]

AWARD PLAQUES

Use these handsome plaques to recognize achievement or service. Shield-shaped plaque of walnut measures 7½″ x 6¼″, has Indianhead design, plate for engraving. Rectangular laminated plaque, 6″ x 9¼″, shows "Higher Vision" color illustration against gray background. Message expresses appreciation for O. A. service.
[E] No. 5068 . . . . **$4.95**
[F] No. 3782 . . . . 1.00

[E]

[F]